WALKER R.N.

The Greatest U-Boat Hunter of the
Battle of the Atlantic
The story of Captain Frederic John
Walker, CB, DSO and three Bars, RN

Terence Robertson

SAPERE
BOOKS

WALKER R.N.

Published by Sapere Books.

24 Trafalgar Road, Ilkley, LS29 8HH

United Kingdom

saperebooks.com

ISBN: 978-1-80055-821-2.

To EILLEEN,
for her fortitude
and high sense of duty,
and to
All those mothers and wives who
influenced so greatly the spirit
of our fighting men at sea

TABLE OF CONTENTS

FOREWORD

by

Admiral Sir Alexander Madden, KCB, CBE, RN

Captain Frederic John Walker, Royal Navy, was a forthright and practical man — full of faith and action in everything he undertook.

We happened to be serving together at the time when he heard that he had not been selected for promotion to captain. He suffered great disappointment: but he met this problem without visible distress and in the same uncompromising way that he met — and overcame — all problems in his naval career.

I feel sure that his countless naval friends would wish me to record our joy — for it was nothing less than that — when his superlative work was, later, regarded with total acclaim.

This book illumines his remarkable character and personality. To those in the Royal Navy who, like myself, were privileged to know him well, there seemed to be nothing missing from his armoury of qualities: he was a high-principled, courageous, modest and kindly naval officer, who looked exactly what he was — an outstanding leader of men.

It would be an impertinence for me to try to add to the great tributes paid to him by famous war leaders. But as a contemporary of his, I am indeed happy to have this chance of recalling the deep admiration and affection in which, over many years, I held this unforgettable youth and man. His place in naval history is assured.

INTRODUCTION

For five and a half years the Battle of the Atlantic raged with ruthless and varying intensity — 'the most protracted and bitterly fought campaign in which the British Empire and her Allies have ever been engaged'.[1] On its outcome depended our power to continue the war even on the defensive; our ability to provide raw materials for war production; arms, ammunition and reinforcements for our armies in Burma, Africa, Italy and, later, Normandy; fuel, planes and bombs for the great air offensive against the Reich itself; food and clothing for the Home Front.

In the beginning, the U-boat captains held the initiative. Brilliantly directed by Admiral Karl Doenitz, they took a heavy toll of our shipping. Of the 21 million tons of Allied shipping, totalling more than 4,500 ships, lost during the war, 15 million tons, or 2,775 ships, were sunk by U-boats. The Allies retaliated by 'killing' 781 German U-boats, the Royal Navy and RAF Coastal Command aircraft being responsible for the destruction of 80 per cent.

Until the very end the U-boat Arm fought with discipline and efficiency. There was no relaxation of effort, no hesitation to incur risks. On the very night of Germany's surrender they sank three ships on our doorstep, two merchant ships in the Firth of Forth and a minesweeper in Lyme Bay.

At a time when this offensive spirit was at its peak and the U-boats had launched their major attacks, the fears of the War Cabinet were reflected in the Operations Room at the

---

[1] Admiralty statement, 1946.

Admiralty where a large graph occupied nearly one wall. It was divided near the top by a thin red line — a permanent measure of the narrow gap between victory and defeat.

While the rate of sinkings at sea stayed below the line, Britain could survive and fight; once it went above, we could not stay in the war and there would have been only one decision to make. How to surrender with honour?

For many anxious months during the first four years of the war the graph nudged dangerously against the red line, providing staff officers with a cold, mathematical mirror of the struggle on the heaving, flaming waters of the Atlantic battlefield. Then the gap began to widen, almost imperceptibly at first, but at a quickening rate until it became certain that the battle had passed its peak, and the graph was now sliding downwards to statistical safety.

There was nothing accidental about this; no strange fortune of war, no inexplicable blunder on the part of the enemy. It was the direct result of the new offensive tactics of the Navy's 'little ships', largely inspired by the brilliant exploits and untiring efforts of one man who, according to the Admiralty, 'did more to free the Atlantic of the U-boat menace than any other single officer'.

This was the late Captain Frederic John Walker, RN, Companion of the Order of the Bath and holder of the DSO and three Bars — the second naval officer to earn this high award four times.

'Johnnie' Walker possessed probably more than a normal share of two great gifts — faith and curiosity; not the faith of mere credulity, nor the curiosity expressed by a turn of the neck, but each requiring the highest form of courage. If Walker's character had not included the curiosity to find out how to combat U-boats, and the faith to carry into effect his own ideas, the Atlantic battle would certainly have been prolonged and might have taken a very different course.

This is implied in an Admiralty communique issued in 1950, five and a half years after his death, which listed the Navy's greatest wartime achievements.

> Captain Walker, more than any other, won the Battle of the Atlantic. His methods had amazing success and more than any other factor gave the Royal Navy supremacy. It is only now that we have learned the full impact he had on the enemy. No tribute could be too high for the work he carried out.
>
> This ace killer of submarines not only showed what mastery in this art could do, but by his example infected all those others concerned with him in this business with the same enthusiasm.
>
> His death was directly attributable to the overstrain which he suffered in setting that admirable example.

Today, memories of Walker and his striking force are undimmed by time. To those who knew him best, close friends, relatives and brother officers, he is still vividly alive, and I am deeply grateful to them all for their kind assistance given so readily in spite of some memories being as painful as many more were gay and exciting.

In addition to Mrs Walker, who gave me so much of her time and allowed me full use of her late husband's documents and photographs, I must express particular gratitude to Admiral of the Fleet Sir George Creasy, Commander-in-Chief, Portsmouth; the late Admiral Sir Percy Noble, former Commander-in-Chief, Western Approaches; Captain E. Hastlehurst, RN (Retd); Captain Donald MacIntyre, RN (Retd); Captain P. J. Cooper, RN (Retd); Captain W. B. Walker, RN (Retd); Commander D. E. G. Wemyss, RN Retd), for permission to refer to his book *Walker's Groups in the Western Approaches*, published by the *Liverpool Daily Post and Echo*, Mrs Georgina Forbes, Captain Walker's eldest sister; Lieutenant-Commander J. S. Filleul, RN; Lieutenant H. W. F. Johnson, RNVR, and Lieutenant Alan Burn, RNVR, who unselfishly allowed me full use of his own unpublished memoirs on which he toiled for many years in the hope that one day they would appear as a tribute to his late captain.

Those members of the Admiralty who devoted so much time to ensure that necessary documents were at all times available to me — Mr C. H. Hurford, Miss D. Johnson and their colleagues in the Historical Section; Mr I. Jerome, of the Department of Naval Information; Mr Elmers, Chief of the Records Office; Commander M. C. Saunders, RN (Retd), head of the Foreign Documents Section; Mr E. Thompson, of the Scrutiny Section, and Mr W. Parry, of the Photographic Library.

I must express particular gratitude to Their Lordships of the Board of Admiralty for their ready consent that I should receive full facilities for the inspection of documents.

Victory has been won and should be won by such as he. May there never be wanting in this realm a succession of men of like spirit in discipline, imagination and valour, humble and unafraid. Not dust nor the light weight of stone, but all the sea of the Western Approaches shall be his tomb.

ADMIRAL SIR MAX HORTON

CHAPTER I: EARLY YEARS

Mr Midshipman Frederic John Walker, RN, former King's Medallist at the Royal Naval College, Dartmouth, contemporary of the late King George VI, and lately star cadet in the training ship HMS *Cornwall*, walked across the gangway from the pier at Plymouth and boarded the battleship HMS *Ajax*, It was a glorious June day in 1914 and the gold-lacquered buttons on his midshipman's patches gleamed as he saluted the quarterdeck, reported to the Officer of the Day and joined his first Gunroom Mess.

The next day, *Ajax* left harbour and sailed for Scapa Flow to observe with the Second Battle Squadron of the Grand Fleet. Mr Midshipman Walker, aged eighteen to the month, had gone to war.

He joined *Ajax* with a formidable background of high marks for his courses as a cadet. Captain Hodges, the strict but fair-minded commanding officer of the training cruiser, had passed him out with a 'Very Good' for engineering, navigation, pilotage, gunnery, torpedo and electrical work and then spoiled the report somewhat by awarding only a 'Good' for seamanship. But he made up for it by rounding off the training period with a report which said: 'He has shown good attention to his work and his conduct has been very good.' This was no mean tribute, as 'VG' is the highest award possible during this part of a young officer's career.

This brilliance in theoretical naval education — he had passed out top of his class at Dartmouth — was matched by natural qualities of leadership. He could pass an examination without apparent effort; as Cadet Captain, he could control a class of rowdy cadets, who had a healthy respect for his ability in the boxing ring and on the rugger field.

His father, Captain Frederic Murray Walker, RN, was astonished at this record, for Johnnie, the second son in a family of three brothers and four sisters had, until the age of ten or eleven, shown less favourable tendencies. When on holiday he would burst into tears if school were mentioned or when the time came to return.

Dartmouth had knocked any tendency to tears out of him, and he had found it a waste of time trying to be too tough with boys quite capable of looking after themselves.

In *Ajax* the fact that there was a war on was in no way allowed to interfere with the next stage to be faced by all 'Snotties'. By the time promotion grew near he had earned the maximum number of marks and, in addition, was four times credited with being a 'clever, reliable and hard-working officer'.

In the spring of 1915, Eilleen Stobart, the attractive, darkhaired young daughter of a well-known North Country family, sat with her cousin, Melissa Laurence, in their home at Etherley, Co. Durham, knitting for friends in the Services. Melissa's pair of mittens was to be sent to her brother Guy, then a midshipman in *Ajax*, while Eilleen was not sure who should become the proud owner of her pair of socks. Suddenly, she exclaimed: 'Melissa, you know that midshipman called Johnnie Walker who Guy is always talking about, the tall one who did so well at Dartmouth.... We saw him at a dance at the Darwins, but Guy wouldn't introduce him to me because he said Walker wouldn't want to be bothered with a flapper? Let's send him our knitting. He's in *Ajax* now. And it will spike Guy's guns for being so boring at the dance.'

Melissa fell in with the idea and, some days later, on board *Ajax* an enraged and somewhat embarrassed midshipman drew

Walker to one side in the Gunroom and said: 'There's a parcel addressed to you from an awful cousin of mine. I shouldn't take the slightest notice of it if I were you.'

But Johnnie felt differently, and after he had opened the parcel a cautious correspondence sprang up between Etherley and the various ports round Britain called at by *Ajax*. In January 1916 he was promoted to sub-lieutenant and in June transferred to a smaller ship, HMS *Mermaid*, then based at Dover.

This was his chance. Eilleen received a letter suggesting that, as he would soon be able to spend a day in London, she might care to join him. She wangled permission to visit friends in London and they met one afternoon for tea at Rumpelmayers.

Several large cream buns vanished before they overcame mutual shyness sufficiently for Johnnie to suggest an evening out. Eilleen would have been furious if he hadn't, and they dined at the Savoy, saw a show afterwards and Johnnie reluctantly caught the last train to Dover.

A few days later, he spent a short leave at Etherley during which the young lovers sought to escape the family by sitting hidden in the strawberry bed with Eilleen's Siamese cat acting as a disinterested 'gooseberry'. After two or three further meetings, they became unofficially and most secretly engaged.

Until then, Eilleen had been in no particular hurry to marry, but she found in the tall, athletic, six-foot-odd sub-lieutenant with the wide shoulders, rather gaunt face and crinkly, dark brown hair, a boyish charm utterly lacking in her other boy friends. He was shy without being timid, straightforward and reserved without being dull. Above all, he was quite obviously and deeply in love with her. The engagement had to be kept quiet as tentative soundings on the depths of her father's feelings on naval officers as potential sons-in-law found bottom rapidly when he declared that Eilleen was too young to marry; so was Johnnie, and a sub-lieutenant's pay was barely enough for one soul, let alone to sustain a wife and possibly a family. The romance continued undaunted but under cover.

Johnnie had been moved again, this time to the destroyer *Sarpedon*, and with him went a reputation for being a young officer of set convictions which he stubbornly refused to discard. This had not been an asset in big ships, where there were far too many people all willing to argue and very much senior. Captain Walker had said of his second son: 'That boy will argue the hind leg off a donkey.' This was not always wise if the 'donkey' were senior enough to put an indifferent note into a sub-lieutenant's confidential report.

Johnnie joined *Sarpedon* with relief — from now on the Navy for him would consist of nothing but destroyers, nothing larger or smaller. Their Lordships had other ideas.

Sub-lieutenant Walker was completely happy in *Sarpedon*. She was employed in screening the Grand Fleet against submarine attack, and this provided him with a new interest in anti-submarine warfare, a subject that was to absorb and fascinate him for the remainder of his life.

While still in this destroyer he was promoted to lieutenant and, reinforced by the extra wealth from the second stripe, he persuaded Eilleen to bring their romance to the surface in the hope that her family would refrain from torpedoing it out of hand. His own father, who had been recalled to duty for the duration, had been sent home on indefinite sick leave and raised no objections to the proposed marriage. Neither did Eilleen's father, though what had happened between 1916 and 1918 to alter the position escaped them both. Even on a lieutenant's pay they could only look forward to a meagre time. Mr Stobart did, however, qualify his blessing by telling a friend:

'Two silly young fools, I think. Both have got comfortable homes. Why the hell do they want to leave them?'

For John, the homeless wanderings of a sailor were no new experience. His mother, four sisters, two brothers and himself had moved about regularly, packing and unpacking according to the movements of their father. He had been born in Plymouth and then moved to a variety of towns stretching from the South Coast to Scotland; of these, they stayed longest in Milford-on-Sea and Bath, which became their last home town as a family.

Then, not long before the wedding, Captain Walker's illness became serious and, while being nursed by his wife in Bath, he collapsed and died. However, the Walker family was contributing two-thirds of its sons to the Navy; for John's elder brother was now Lieutenant William Baggot Walker, RN, and the youngest had also tried to enter, only to be turned down because his eyesight was too weak.

They married with Bill Walker[2] as best man and, after a brief honeymoon at Bournemouth, Eilleen settled down to the nomadic life of a naval officer's wife. In the first year they stayed nowhere long enough to set up a home. While John returned for a spell in big ships as a watchkeeper in the battleship *Valiant*, Eilleen moved around, leaving behind a dismal trail of hotel rooms and flats. But they were supremely happy and, like all young lovers, completely confident of the future.

With John at sea, Eilleen stayed for a while with his mother in Bath. It was here on March 22nd, 1920, that she gave birth to their first child, Timothy.

---

[2] Five years later Bill Walker, now Captain W. B. Walker, RN (Retd), married Eilleen's youngest sister, Peggy.

During his next leave, John told his wife of his impatience with the strict discipline and social life that was a normal part of battleship routine and confessed he was trying to have himself transferred back to destroyers. He was still keen on learning more about anti-submarine tactics and had decided that, if he specialized in this field, he would greatly enhance his chances of serving in small anti-submarine ships, which he would also like. The few shillings a day 'specialist's allowance' was a further attraction. He volunteered for a new and special course at Portland naval base where a school of anti-submarine warfare had been recently established, called HMS *Osprey*.

A year later, his request for transfer was accepted and he left *Valiant* for Portland to begin his technical courses on secret equipment prior to becoming a specialist.

During the next four years Lieutenant and Mrs Walker managed to establish a temporary base in adjacent Weymouth, not daring to make it too permanent in case sailing orders arrived. Ready money was an urgent problem indeed, and sometimes Johnnie was forced to look around for something to sell. On one occasion when he was in Portsmouth and Eilleen in Weymouth, there was the chance of a week-end together. Eilleen counted up the housekeeping and decided she would have to stay in Weymouth. Johnnie discovered he had seven and sixpence to spare after paying his mess bill, hardly enough for a week-end with his family. His eyes strayed to an expensive-looking travelling clock they had received as a wedding present. He would pawn it — but first it needed repairing. He took it to a watchmaker and, on the eve of his free week-end, collected the clock, instructed the shop to send the bill on to him, and marched straight round to a pawnshop. He hoped for twenty-five bob, perhaps two pounds.

The pawnbroker offered seven and six. Argument was useless, it was seven and six or nothing. John pocketed the three half crowns ruefully. It would be enough to reach Weymouth. But the following morning the repair bill arrived. He had expected it to be two or three shillings at the most. It cost the enormous sum of twelve and sixpence. John fingered the fifteen shillings in his pocket. Later in the day, he paid the bill and wired Eilleen that he was staying in Portsmouth minus clock and with five shillings less than when he had first thought of pawning it.

It was characteristic of the young couple that, although frequently hard up, they were never in debt. Johnnie would draw his last penny from the bank to buy Eilleen some unexpected gift, but kept a tight rein on bills. He never worried about money; when it was short he would say — 'Everything will turn out all right' — and it always did.

The Walker trio, father, mother and son, matured and learned to cope with recurrent minor financial crises. Father, always an individualist, acquired the reputation of being an outspoken critic of instruction he considered ill-advised or based on wrong precepts. Yet he was a popular figure at *Osprey* and regarded as one of the few pioneer experts in the developing art of tactical defence and attack against an underwater enemy.

Mrs Walker increased her authority over all things domestic by giving birth in 1924 to a second son, Nicholas, and a year later to their first daughter, Gillian.

But the years ashore made Walker restless, even promotion to lieutenant-commander failing to induce him to settle down in his career. For many long hours, he discussed with his wife the attractive possibility of leaving the Navy and finding a more lucrative job in civilian life while they were both young.

When he said that the Navy in peacetime was 'not my cup of tea' he really meant it. He had enormous energy and an equally vast capacity for sheer hard work, but the Navy had returned to its pre-War role of providing a salty atmosphere in society ashore.

Overshadowing this frustrating state of affairs was Walker's awareness that a healthy and growing family would tax his income to the limit. He was a family man and hated to think that the number of children he might enjoy could be limited by naval pay. For a long time he toyed with the possibility of seeing how much farther his economy would stretch outside the Navy. Eilleen, however, knew he would never really be happy outside the Service and gently opposed his most determined decisions to make a change.

He burned away most of this excess energy in gardening, hockey, swimming and boxing, if and when someone at *Osprey* was brash enough to suggest a round or two in the gym. He had given up rugger, although he might easily have played for the Navy, but was still a nimble middleweight with a powerful punch in both fists. But his speed, offensive spirit and individuality emerged best on the hockey field where he played himself into the Dorset county eleven and would have been selected for the West of England team but for a capricious Appointments Branch of the Admiralty which decided at that moment to send him back to sea.

Further thoughts of leaving the Navy were pushed aside, and he left Portland to serve for the next five years in the battleships *Revenge*, *Nelson* and *Queen Elizabeth* as Fleet Anti-Submarine Officer of the Atlantic and Mediterranean fleets.

This period in what he regarded as floating parade grounds, where no one from admirals downward seemed to care much about submarines or their antidotes, was punctuated by continual but fruitless efforts to have himself transferred back to destroyers. The only bright spot came in the Mediterranean when he outpointed a mountainous sailor to become unofficial middleweight champion of the Fleet.

Although a brilliant future had been predicted for him at Dartmouth, Walker came face to face with the sudden realization that he had entered the zone for promotion to commander, passed through most of it and had only a few months left before he would become 'passed over' as a lieutenant-commander. Not even a 'brass-hat' to show for all that early promise.

He tackled his senior officers, finally reaching the Commander-in-Chief, Mediterranean, whose reply was hardly encouraging. But, not long afterwards, he received the third ring of a commander with an appointment to take command of the destroyer. *Shikari*, 'brain' of the Navy's first radio-controlled gunnery target ship, *Centurion*. The Navy had never looked better to Commander Walker. His ship was equipped with the latest asdic[3] and other anti-submarine devices. At home, the extra pay made him feel almost affluent.

Unfortunately, the *Shikari* days ended all too soon and six months later he learned with dismay that he was to be sent to the China Station to take command of the sloop *Falmouth*, also used by the Commander-in-Chief, Far Eastern Fleet, as his personal yacht. He remarked tersely to his wife 'I know I'm not cut out for that job.'

---

[3] This device enabled surface ships to detect submerged submarines. It sent out sound waves underwater which produced a distinctive 'ping' or echo, if they hit metallic objects. As it also produced echoes from shoals of fish, wrecks and confused whirlpools of water, the operator had to be highly trained to distinguish the difference.

Before leaving for China, Eilleen took a personal step she had been considering for some time. Since childhood, religion had meant much to her, and one of Johnnie's attractions had been his belief not only in God, but in going to church. When ashore he attended services every Sunday. Now Eilleen decided to become a Catholic. To remain an Anglican, feeling as she did, would have been to live a lie and she refused to do this even for the sake of husband and family.

Johnnie, eminently fair-minded, put no obstacles in her way, although he preferred to remain in his own religion. Eilleen's conversion was carried out smoothly. On the question of the children, Johnnie was decisive. They were to be allowed to choose for themselves when they were old enough and, until then, would remain in the Anglican Church in which they had been brought up. In return, he agreed that, should they ever have another child, he should be raised as a Catholic.

On Sundays, they walked up the road together, each to go to their respective churches; often, if Johnnie arrived in a port before Eilleen, he would hunt out her church and note the rimes of services for her.

Not long afterwards, he left England for China, an interlude in his career which placed the first black mark against his name in the files of the Admiralty.

CHAPTER 2: NEARLY A FAILURE

IN the years between his arrival at Dartmouth as a boy and the receipt of his orders to proceed to China, Johnnie Walker had not put a foot wrong in the Service. In spite of managing to scrape through to commander only just before the promotion zone passed, his personal record at the Admiralty was good, and it was likely that he would receive promotion at the normal rate, perhaps to Flag rank.

But from the time he joined the Far Eastern Fleet dubious reports on his suitability for senior rank were to be written into an otherwise impeccable record. When the Fleet moved from one part of the China station to another, Johnnie clashed with his superiors. Always outspoken and inclined to put his case with considerable forcefulness, he failed to show the necessary tact in those social duties which go with the command of the Admiral's yacht. When his two years' service abroad were up and he returned to England, adverse reports from a senior officer had already reached London.

He was glad to be back. Eilleen had fallen ill in China and he was anxious to have her examined by London specialists. The result was that she underwent two major operations, while Johnnie was sent to Greenwich for a senior officer's course.

Meanwhile, Timmy, as the family called him, had won a scholarship to Eton and, while there, prepared to enter the Catholic Church. He was only sixteen and Johnnie had not intended his children to choose for themselves at such an early age. However, in the face of the boy's determination, he gave his consent and allowed him to have instruction. As quiet, blunt and forthright as his father, Timothy was received into the Church in July 1936, and later accepted for the priesthood.

Walker had now received his next appointment, as second-in-command of the battleship *Valiant*. Despite his refusal in China to bow to what he regarded as the whims of higher authorities, the harsh reports on him had not been sufficient in themselves seriously to affect his career. But while in *Valiant* there came another clash of personalities which led to one more adverse report.

In recent years, a great change had taken place in Walker; from a home-loving boy he had become a gifted scholar and hero to his classmates; and now the young naval officer had grown into a mature, somewhat serious-minded father and deeply devoted husband. Gone were the youthful days of early marriage when gay cocktail parties with his young wife had been accompanied by occasional visits to the pawnbroker's. They were replaced by a supreme contentment only to be found when at home playing with the children and in peaceful evenings with Eilleen. His family possessed him and he was only too willing to be possessed. This was encouraged, perhaps, by the Admiralty's persistent refusal to appoint him to the small ships he liked, sending him instead to one big ship after another.

He had developed a tolerant understanding of the problems and worries besetting officers who were following the modern trend of marrying while young and accepting the challenge of making ends meet on Service pay. He had been through it himself and could now draw upon his own experience and happiness when giving advice.

It used to be — and to some extent still is — an accepted naval maxim that a career officer can have only one wife, the Navy; if he takes another she must be relegated to second place. Walker came up against this in *Valiant*. The commander of a battleship has one of the most arduous, responsible and absorbing jobs the Navy can offer. If the captain is the king, then the commander, as the senior executive officer, is his prime minister. He controls the lives of nearly 2,000 men; administers their duties, their leaves and their pay; he cares for their health, punishes their sins, rewards their virtues, helps those in trouble and maintains sanity in conditions often suitable to the breeding of abnormality. He is responsible to the captain for the training of officers and men and the fighting efficiency and cleanliness of the ship. Round the clock, he is the buffer between the captain and his subject community. On top of all this, he must be ready at an instant's notice to take overall command should the captain fall sick, wounded or dead.

Johnnie Walker performed his duties in *Valiant* adequately. She was as good as any ship of the line in the Fleet — no better and no worse. This seemed to irritate her captain who relied, understandably, on his commander to pull that extra effort from the crew to make her that little bit smarter, with just that fine shade of efficiency which carries the stamp of a keen, untiring executive officer.

Sharp words were exchanged at frequent intervals and Johnnie would return to his cabin to find solace in writing letters to Eilleen and the children. He wrote every evening and in one letter said: 'I don't think there is the vaguest chance of my being promoted out of this ship.' Yet had anyone suggested that by allowing his wife to occupy first place in his thoughts he had excluded the Navy to a dangerous degree and was, perhaps, not quite producing that little extra effort required of him, he would either have laughed aloud or angrily refuted the charge.

However, the painful fact remained that his captain was married to the Navy in the traditional sense while he was married to Eilleen. Neither officer, with the best will on both sides, could do much to avoid the final encounter.

When Walker left *Valiant* early in 1937, he knew that more criticisms of his ability had reached the Admiralty; in fact, one confidential report described him as 'lacking powers of leadership'. This was a damning judgement when he was entering the zone of promotion to captain. It gave the lie to the natural qualities of leadership he had displayed at Dartmouth and rankled because he felt that, left alone in small ships, he could make as good a leader as anyone.

Yet there was some justification for discrediting him, just as there was reason enough for him to feel that his efforts in *Valiant* had not been fairly valued. Had the Admiralty thought fit to give him a small ship then, his career might have taken a different course, but one appointment after another to big ships had frustrated his sense of adventure and deadened ambition. If he turned to his marriage as the only star in his life one can hardly blame him.

Once he had left *Valiant* all grievances vanished. What was done was finished, and he no longer worried about it. He was disappointed at not being promoted out of the battleship and it began to look as though he would never reach the rank of captain. With a wife and three children, it would have been quite natural for him to worry about the future; instead he was content to let matters take their course, confident that he could always earn a living outside the Service. When Eilleen raised the matter sometimes he would pat her shoulder, and mutter his formula for everything: 'It will all turn out all right, don't you worry.'

In the spring of 1937, he returned to Portland to become commander of the Anti-Submarine Warfare School, HMS *Osprey*. This was work he liked, but there was an ominous cloud in the sky. It was becoming increasingly obvious to the pioneers of this form of warfare that the majority of senior officers regarded their work as necessary but not of high importance. Other branches of the Service offered more glamour, and it seemed likely that the anti-submarine specialists might easily be overlooked for promotion — another signpost which Walker merely ignored.

In September, Timmy left Eton to join the English College in Rome for preliminary training as a priest, while his father plunged into his work at *Osprey* with one ear attuned to the war drums sounding across the Channel on the borders of Germany. He discussed the possible outcome of a war and revealed weak powers of prophecy.

'I think,' said Eilleen, 'that if the war lasts long enough someone will build an atom bomb. That will be terrible.'

'Oh, forget that,' replied Johnnie amiably. 'They haven't reached anything like that stage yet.'

Those were good days for the Walkers, among the happiest Eilleen can remember. They had a house called 'The Four Winds' which the children adored because it had a tennis court, though they spent most of their time fishing from a nearby stone pier, catching slimy creatures which father and mother then had to eat.

On one sunny afternoon, while Johnnie was gardening, Gillian turned the hose on him and then wilted under a paternal broadside. She promptly christened her father 'Beetroot', because 'his face went all red and he shouted at me in a gunnery voice'. The nickname stuck to the end.

Not long afterwards Johnnie bought his first car, very old and dilapidated, but still mobile. Before going to Dorchester one day for his driving test, Nicholas, who had silently observed his father's driving for several days, asked anxiously if he thought he would pass.

'Of course,' replied Johnnie, a little coldly. 'If I can drive a destroyer, I can drive a bloody car.'

The family kept tactfully out of the way an hour or so later when he returned to confess that, after an argument with the examiner on the necessity of using hand signals, indicators or both, he had been failed.

By the end of 1938, Commander Walker knew he had not been selected for promotion and had joined the ranks of those who, for a variety of reasons, had been 'passed over'. In peacetime, these officers can either elect to remain in the Service at their existing rank until reaching maximum retiring age, or retire at the first opportunity, thereby gaining a small pension while still young enough to supplement it by employment in Civvy Street. In wartime, however, 'passed over' officers were often called upon to fill posts of importance — and in many cases they did so brilliantly. As if in compensation, Eilleen gave birth, in March 1939, to a third son whom they named Andrew.

In *Osprey* Walker insisted that the U-boat menace would soon become the key to Britain's defence and power to attack. No matter what the beliefs of higher authorities, he urged the commanding officer of the school to press his view on the Admiralty. Whether this was done is not known, but his next appointment was one of the most important in the Navy's anti-submarine defence system. He became Staff Officer (Operations) on the staff of Vice-Admiral Ramsay at Dover with overall responsibility for the Command's anti-submarine defences.

With the BEF in France, freedom of movement in the Channel was vital for the supply lines. It was also essential to deny use of the Channel to U-boats moving from the German ports of Kiel, Bremen and Wilhelmshaven into the Atlantic. By forcing them to take the northern route round the Orkneys, we could make them use more fuel on their outward and inward voyages which meant less time on Atlantic patrols against our convoys. Therefore, the closing of the Dover-Calais door in the face of Doenitz was the task of a highly-trained specialist. Walker himself was disappointed at the appointment. Although it lifted him from the list of the 'virtually unemployed' and gave him an active, key role in the front line of events, he would have preferred command of a small ship.

They had moved most of their belongings and furniture into store at Weymouth and taken a furnished house in Dover, when a letter arrived for Johnnie from Timmy, who had been in Rome for the past two years. It was a remarkable letter, laying bare the mental agony of a boy, then nineteen, who had given himself to his faith at a time when his country had gone to war. He now sought advice and guidance from his father.

After explaining that he was not free to return and fight as he chose, Timmy said he had talked the matter over with his rector and that, as a Church student, he would have first to obtain the permission of Cardinal Hinsley, Archbishop of Westminster, before joining up for the duration.

> As far as my personal inclinations are concerned [he wrote] I would much rather fight than stay here. To go on with my ordinary work while England is at war would involve deep mortification and require far greater courage. But I am

determined not to act upon inclination, but to try simply to find out what is right.

The reasons which urge me to fight are too obvious to be expounded at length. It is a conflict in which everything which has any claim on my loyalty is involved — Church, Country and civilization itself.

The reasons against it are such that I must ask you to adjudge them with that appreciation of my position as a Catholic which you have hitherto so generously shown. I have already said that the Church disapproves of it. The reason is that the vocation to priesthood is the highest of all vocations, higher even than the vocation to fight for your country and it is more important, not only for the Church but also for England to have good priests rather than to have good soldiers or sailors.

To leave the Church even for a few years to fight for a cause, however just, unless the number of Church students were so great as to make a vital difference — which it is not — would be to prefer the gratification of a romantic impulse to doing my real duty to my Country and my Church — a most un-English thing to do.

Before coming to a final conclusion I want you to tell me what in your opinion it is my duty to do. Because you probably do not want to influence my decision I must make it clear I am determined not to be influenced. I realize that I alone am responsible before my Church and my Country and cannot shift it on to anyone else.

Walker replied at once that Timmy was to stay in Rome, but should there ever come a time when England would need every able-bodied man, then he would write and say so. It would be up to his son to make his own decision. There, the matter rested.

International developments took a hand. Italy attacked France, and the English College in Rome was disbanded for the duration, the English students returning home by sea to wait until the College could find suitable accommodation to reopen in England. Timothy joined his mother and father in Dover and, throughout the evacuation of Dunkirk, worked as a stretcher-bearer at Dover Hospital.

The English College re-opened in the Lake District and Timothy left Dover to resume his studies. But, shortly afterwards, his father sent the promised letter. In Johnnie's opinion, the time had come when every fit man was needed to fight the war. Timothy obtained his rector's consent to write to Cardinal Hinsley asking for permission to suspend his studies for the priesthood until the end of the war, in order to join one of the Fighting Services.

There was no delay in the reply. It came almost at once.

My dear Mr Walker, — Your letter shows you have a thoroughly Catholic and patriotic disposition.

I agree that you should join one of the Fighting Services. It is sad and deplorable that you should have to interrupt your studies. But you will probably come out of the ordeal a stronger man and by God's grace, make a more useful priest. I do not think you can oppose your father's wish.

My heartfelt Blessing,
Yours devotedly in Christ,
A. Cardinal Hinsley

Timothy packed his bags, caught a train to London and joined the Royal Naval Volunteer Reserve as an ordinary seaman. With young Nicholas already at Dartmouth, the Walkers could be proud of their sons.

CHAPTER 3: WAR COMMAND

The struggle to secure a sea appointment after Dunkirk proved more difficult than Walker had thought possible. The Battle of Britain was fought and won largely within sight and hearing of his office at Dover Castle; the threat of a German invasion provided a temporary outlet for his restless mind as he played his role in preparing the South Coast's defences. Then came another and far more serious menace. The U-boats, already individually successful, devised their 'wolf pack' attacks and massacred convoys left burning trails across the seas.

The peril he had planned for, and against which he had continuously warned at the Anti-Submarine School, made him increasingly impatient with Dover as his most responsible job in the war. With reports of increased losses at sea, he began to bombard Admiral Ramsay and Their Lordships with pleas which all rebounded with the curt, official reply: 'Request not approved'.

With every refusal, Walker became more determined to get back to sea. Had there been no war, he would have been content to remain a 'passed over' commander. His principal source of joy was Eilleen and the family; his needs were few, a comfortable home, a garden and sufficient money to give the children a reasonable education. But the moment Britain stood with her back to the sea wall, he impatiently threw aside dreams of a semi-retired existence. This was understood and shared by Eilleen, who realized that any attempt to keep him at home would be selfish. She was quietly prepared to let him find his own place in the fight.

When the shelling of Dover became fierce, his promise that their fourth child should be brought up as a Catholic was remembered. In a letter to his executors, he said:

> Please note the fact that I wish my third son, Andrew, to be brought up and educated as a Roman Catholic. Please ensure that this is done in the event of my death.

In March 1941, he travelled to London on leave and called at the Admiralty to see an old friend, Captain George Creasy,[4] then Director of Anti-Submarine Warfare. Creasy was one of the few men who knew how badly the Battle of the Atlantic was going, how serious were our losses and how necessary it was to have the best men and equipment sent to Liverpool, the new headquarters of the Western Approaches Command. He knew Walker as an anti-submarine specialist: the fact that his friend had been passed over meant only that he had suffered in the cut-throat competition for a place on the pre-war promotion list. Here was a man who should be usefully employed in the grim struggle at sea.

He listened to Walker's arguments for a sea command and ended the interview by promising to do everything within his power. This was not too great, but sufficient for him to be able to write a personal letter to the Commander-in-Chief, Western Approaches, Admiral Sir Percy Noble, outlining Walker's qualifications and recommending a command.

It is inevitable in war that the customs of peace often get kicked out of the window. If at this time the Admiralty took a little longer to start kicking, it was only because its deeply ingrained customs were fundamentally good ones. We were

---

[4] Later Admiral of the Fleet Sir George Creasy, Commander-in-Chief, Portsmouth.

losing more ships than we could hope to build, and one of the first customs to suffer was the practice of keeping 'passed over' officers in subordinate positions. Experienced officers, particularly those trained in anti-submarine warfare, were in short supply, and an obscure department was ordered to sift personnel. The process was slow but efficient. On receipt of Creasy's letter, Sir Percy Noble started the machine to have Walker transferred from Dover to his own Command. In September, the Admiralty sent a signal to Dover which ordered him to Liverpool to assume command of HMS *Stork* for duties in the Atlantic under the Commander-in-Chief, Western Approaches.

The next few days were filled with contented excitement for the Walker family. Ordinary Seaman Timothy had been selected as a candidate for a commission in the RNVR and had been sent to an officers' training unit; Cadet Nicholas of Dartmouth had become Mr Midshipman Walker awaiting a sea posting; Gillian had another year at school before she could fulfil her ambition to join the Wrens; and Commander and Mrs Walker handed in the lease of the house they had rented at Dover for more than a year, waved farewell to less fortunate friends who had to stay in a town still being bombed and under daily fire from the long-range guns of Calais, and set off for separate destinations — Mrs Walker to her family at Hambledon, near Henley, and her husband to Liverpool to take over his own ship and prepare her to meet the enemy wherever he could be found.

After months of office work at Dover, where extensive minefields were relied upon to deny the Channel passage to U-boats, bustling Liverpool presented an exciting, warlike contrast. This great seaport and frontline base of our Atlantic operations teemed with industry as stevedores raced to unload and load the stream of dirty, unpainted freighters; cranes clattered in the docks while pneumatic drills throbbed in the repair yards; tugs scurried urgently up and down the wide Mersey, their whistles bleating anxiously; sleek destroyers, busy sloops and bouncy, brash corvettes marched and countermarched along swept channels cleared by patient minesweepers.

Among the massive, smoke-blackened buildings lining the waterfront was Derby House, a comparatively new office block now transformed into the headquarters of Admiral Sir Percy Noble who, little more than a year before, had set up his Command to ensure the 'safe and timely arrival of our convoys'. When he arrived with his Chief of Staff, Commodore J. M. Mansfield, and the Air Officer Commanding No 19 Group of Coastal Command, he had only the promise of ships and men. The Admiralty had scoured the coasts and seas until the Western Approaches Command now controlled the destinies of thousands of men sailing from Gibraltar to Murmansk, from New York to the Channel.

A vast headquarters organization tracked each convoy and Escort Group round the clock; the Intelligence Division intercepted enemy wireless signals at sea to pin-point the positions of every known U-boat; the Air Staff sent their aircraft along the convoy routes to the PLE — Prudent Limit of Endurance, the point at which they must turn back if remaining fuel was to last out.

Into this organization stepped Walker who at once found himself among strangely assorted bedfellows. It seemed that by design or accident all the misfits of the Navy had congregated at Liverpool. Among his brother officers were many of his own kind — 'passed overs' who at some stage or other had become red-tape rebels. But the vast majority were officers of the Royal Naval Volunteer Reserve, week-end sailors churned out by the recruiting machine often with inadequate training. The Royal Naval Reserve, those independent merchant men who would become sore boils in big ship wardrooms, somehow fitted in here by providing their expert seamanship to balance the ignorance of the willing, but lamentably 'green', RNVR.

A generous variety of these officers manned the ships of the 36th Escort Group when Walker took command of His Majesty's sloop *Stork*, and became to his surprise and delight the senior officer of the Group's nine ships which consisted in addition to *Stork*, of the sloop *Deptford*, and the corvettes *Rhododendron*, *Marigold*, *Convolvulus*, *Penstemon*, *Gardenia*, *Samphire* and *Vetch*.

His first job was to find out something about the eight commanding officers serving under him, and try out the ships' companies. All told, upwards of five hundred men who had never before set eyes on each other had to become a trained, well-knit team. This was the key to Walker's personal plan; if U-boats were to be destroyed, the hunters would have to become a team, with himself as its playing manager. As the Group left harbour bound for working-up exercises, Walker was grimly determined that each of the individualists astern of him would quickly learn that the 36th Group was to be a unit welded in one cause — the destruction of the enemy.

The working-up routine had been skilfully devised by an expert in the art of driving both officers and men mad in the least possible time. All day they carried out anti-submarine and gunnery exercises; at night they sailed again to protect imaginary convoys. When the sleepless days and nights had stretched into weeks, and orders were given and obeyed automatically, they were allowed one night at anchor. Tired out, the Group collapsed into bunks and hammocks. But it was not to be. In the early hours, the energetic senior officer of the training school came alongside in a motor-boat.

'Officer of the Day.'

'Yes, Sir.'

'You have been rammed forward, your stern is on fire and the enemy are preparing to attack the anchorage. Get cracking.'

Alarm bells rang and they were at it again.

By the middle of November, they were about as trained as the brief course would allow. There was some cooperation between ships — not much it is true, but some. There was no time for anything more. Sir Percy needed every ship on the Atlantic runs.

A few days later, the Group returned to Liverpool and reported ready for duty. Walker himself was not entirely satisfied that they were. The course had provided all concerned with an opportunity to get to know their neighbours, and it had been possible to see how the commanding officers handled their ships. It was also true that, when they took the field, he could now confidently expect them to know in which direction to kick the ball. But sadly, and quite understandably, they were not yet a team.

He felt it urgent that every commanding officer in the Group should know exactly what to do in any emergency; and that every individual move should be related so that each ship was operating to a set plan. He would have to make the plans, and his team — when it became one — could then act accordingly. In fact, with a minimum of reference back they would be doing what he wanted them to do automatically and without waiting for orders.

In the brief moments of relaxation during exercises, he had drawn up a series of orders to his captains which he called,

'36th Escort Group Operational Instructions'. They were succinct, concise and, like Walker himself, direct:

(1) The object of the Group while on escort duty is to ensure the safe and timely arrival of the convoy concerned. It is not possible, with the ships available, to dispose of the Group in such a way as to protect the convoy completely from enemy attacks — these must be accepted and doubtless some losses. The only practicable course of action is to ensure that any enemy craft, either surface or air, which attack are destroyed.

(2) The particular aim of the Group therefore is to be taken as the destruction of any enemy which attacks the convoy. U-boats are the chief menace to our convoys. I cannot emphasise too strongly that a U-boat sighted or otherwise detected is immediately to be attacked continuously without further orders, with guns, depth charges and/or ram until she has been destroyed or until further orders are received.

(3) I wish to impress on all officers that, although I shall naturally take charge of the majority of operations, I consider it essential for themselves to act instantly without waiting for orders in situations of which I may be unaware or imperfectly informed.

(4) It should seldom, if ever, be necessary to conclude a signalled report with the words: 'Request instructions'. Action should be 'proposed' or 'intended' by the men on the spot — and the senior officer can always say if he doesn't like it.

(5) No officer will ever be blamed by me for getting on with the job in hand.

A slight clash with Derby House arose over a plan he had devised for dealing with U-boat attacks on a convoy at night. Using the private family name for his wife, he termed the plan 'Operation Buttercup'. This, in essence, called for turning night into day by a generous use of every form of illuminant such as starshell and rockets.

'It is the practice of U-boats,' he said, 'to attack our convoys at night, operating, trimmed down on the surface. Once the enemy has located a convoy several U-boats are likely to converge and attack at short intervals. Experience shows that, after an attack, the U-boat will either remain near the wreck of a torpedoed ship, or make off on the surface at high speed to escape the attention of slower escorts.

'Operation Buttercup is designed to force the U-boat to dive by plastering the area round the wreck with depth-charges and by illuminating the most likely directions of his surface escape. Once submerged, the destruction of the submarine is considerably simplified. The object of Operation Buttercup therefore is to destroy any U-boat which has succeeded in attacking a convoy escorted by night by this Group.'

The technical method of carrying out this operation so impressed the Operations Staff that a copy was shown to Sir Percy Noble. It was basically sound, but the Commander-in-Chief instructed Walker to make amendments to those clauses with which he did not entirely agree.

Walker obeyed with surprising meekness and in consequence the name 'Buttercup', hitherto reserved by the Walker family, was issued for the guidance of the whole Western Approaches Command with the Derby House endorsement that the operation provided the maximum chance of sinking U-boats at night. Walker had begun to make his presence felt in the battle.

His presence had also been felt in the sturdy little, peace-time-built *Stork*, Ships invariably take on the spirit of their crews: a happy, efficient crew means a buoyant, reliable ship which rarely sees the repair yard and answers willingly to any calls made upon it; a discontented crew — which often means laxity and inefficiency — and the ship is sluggish when she should be fast and ready for that tiny bit extra when most needed. The difference comes from the top — the captain.

Stork had become a happy ship. Walker demanded a lot of his officers and men, but he rarely interfered with his officers on the details of their respective duties. His enthusiasm passed right down to the crew who became increasingly aware of the vital role each man played in the fighting of his ship. The men were keen and *Stork* was happy. She would behave well in battle.

Towards the end of November 1941, the 36th Group sailed from Liverpool to take an outward-bound convoy to Gibraltar. This first trip — a test for them all — was fortunate indeed. A series of heavy gales hit the convoy, driving it into huge seas and howling winds which made it unlikely that U-boats would be operating seriously on the surface. Walker grabbed the chance to put his Group through a series of exercises, gunnery shoots and depth-charge drills which impressed the convoy. By the time they arrived in Gibraltar early the next month, he could congratulate himself on his handling of the Group and feel confidence in their team efficiency. At a meeting of commanding officers in his own ship he offered the toast:

'To the 36th Group and the total destruction of the enemy.'

Next morning they were ordered to patrol the Gibraltar Straits in an effort to hunt down U-boats on passage into the Mediterranean where they were being employed in attacking Malta-bound convoys and in escorting Axis supply ships carrying vital equipment to Rommel in North Africa.

These U-boats were making the passage so easily and causing so much anxiety to the Mediterranean Fleet that Captain Creasy was flown out from London to attend a series of conferences on the Rock. One of the first decisions — in which Captain Creasy had not much faith — was to maintain a hunting force inside the Straits and, to seaward, in the approaches. The 36th Escort Group was awaiting further convoy duties, so Walker received orders to carry out a series of anti-submarine patrols off Gibraltar.

They were a sorry failure. U-boats continued to pass into the Mediterranean and, despite a week of patrolling, Walker and his Group sighted not so much as a periscope, the only asdic echoes proving to be fish.

The Group was called back to harbour, where they refuelled and, on December 14th, sailed to join convoy HG76 for the voyage home to Liverpool. At a conference prior to sailing, Walker was told: 'The enemy has been cutting the Gibraltar convoys to shreds. This is an important convoy and you will be reinforced with ships of the Gibraltar Command. You must arrive as intact as possible.'

At the rendezvous outside Gibraltar, Walker received as escort reinforcements, the destroyers *Blankney*, *Stanley* and *Exmoor*. In addition, the escort included HMS *Audacity*, a former merchant ship converted into a convoy aircraft-carrier. She had a small flight deck and carried about half a dozen tiny Martlet naval fighters. Their job was to patrol round the convoy, searching for surfaced U-boats and to drive off inquisitive Focke-Wulfs, preferably before they had time to work out and dispatch the convoy's position to base. *Audacity* was the first of this type of carrier to serve along the convoy routes.

By dusk on the 14th the convoy, consisting of thirty-two ships, had been sorted into five columns and the escort had spread itself around them in two thinly-held protective screens — one close to the convoy and the other farther away to act as scouts. Walker, in *Stork*, led the way ahead of the convoy on a north-westerly course, only too well aware that it was just a matter of time before they reached the battlefield and at last faced the enemy.

CHAPTER 4: THE FIRST CLASH

Since their autumn offensive began, the U-boats had singled out our Gibraltar convoy routes for a special kind of blitz. For the first time since the war opened, Doenitz had received sufficient cooperation from the Luftwaffe to enable Focke-Wulf bombers to be sent over the Atlantic in search of convoys, their limited range making the Gibraltar routes the most suitable targets. Their mission was to seek out a convoy and then send out a series of wireless reports giving its position, speed and course on which any U-boats in the vicinity could converge and attack as a 'pack'.

There was little we could do about these 'homing' tactics outside the range of shore-based Coastal Command planes unless each convoy was provided with its own aircraft-carrier.

In July 1941, Korvettenkapitan Arend Baumann, aged thirty-seven and an old hand in the Battle of the Atlantic, took command of the new 740-ton, ocean-going *U-131*. She carried fourteen torpedoes, a crew of forty-eight and could stay at sea for about six weeks. Now the two countries were at war, he was certain of Germany's victory and determined to ensure it by making *U-131* the most efficient submarine in the Atlantic.

Whilst they were exercising in the Baltic, the RAF raided Kiel the night his wife started labour pains heralding the arrival of their second child. She could not find a taxi to take her to hospital, but a fire-engine racing to the bombed docks picked her up and rushed her there in time. *U-131*'s short career was made even more eventful in the Baltic when a Russian submarine just missed her with a torpedo and the excitement had barely died down when a sister U-boat, also on exercises, fired a torpedo which passed under *U-131* and exploded a hundred yards away.

U-131 sailed at noon on November 17th and a week later was cruising off Spain. By December 12th she had sunk one merchant ship — expending six of her torpedoes — and had chased a large liner without success. There was high hope that they would be ordered into Lorient in time to be home for Christmas. Doenitz had other ideas, and sent *U-131* to patrol off Gibraltar. It was a deeply depressed U-boat which sighted a convoy late in the afternoon of the 16th and sent out a general alarm to all submarines in the vicinity.

Baumann knew that at least two other U-boats were around somewhere and decided to shadow the convoy by diving from his position ahead, allowing the convoy to pass over him before surfacing astern to make his hourly homing reports for the gathering 'pack'. In the middle of the manoeuvre, his hydrophones broke down and, when he came up to see where he was, the periscope poked up right in the centre of the convoy. Recovering from his surprise, he selected a target and prepared to fire, but for some reason the merchant ship chose that moment to indulge in some accidental, but really impressive, zigzagging to adjust her position in the column. Baumann was forced to call off the attack; instead, he decided to dive deep and get away before being rammed.

That night he surfaced astern, and his call went out for help. Among those who were close enough to answer the summons were *U-434*, commanded by Kapitanleutnant Wolfgang Heyda, and *U-574*, under Oberleutnant zur see Gegnalbach. Both these boats, like *U-131*, were on their first cruise, having left Kiel about the same time in October. They had joined a 'pack' attacking a convoy in the North Atlantic near Halifax, but after being beaten off had headed southwards on a vain search for prey off Spain. They received *U-131*'s wireless reports on the 16th and steamed at full speed to contact the convoy.

At headquarters in Lorient, Doenitz and his staff moved three tiny flags on their operations map, plotted the probable position, course and speed of the convoy and sent signals to four more U-boats well to the north to make all possible speed to intercept. All day during the 16th a Focke-Wulf had been reinforcing *U-131*'s reports with its own, and Doenitz had every reason to believe it possible to deliver a mutilating blow.

The 'pack' was gathering for the kill.

Convoy HG76 was fully aware it had been sighted. At dusk on the 16th, *Stanley* reported sighting two aircraft at visibility distance. No one else was able to spot them, and Walker wrote in his War Diary: 'This report was pooh-poohed by *Audacity*, but *Stanley* stuck stoutly to his convictions. I have assumed the enemy has now passed our full particulars to every U-boat not wearing a deaf-aid.' This was confirmed at midnight by the Admiralty.

When shadowing a convoy, U-boats usually stayed on the surface at visibility distance from the convoy, submerging only when there was a danger of being seen either by aircraft or an inquisitive escort. As they were low in the water, they could keep watch on the convoy's mastheads while relying on their own tiny silhouette to keep them well hidden from the escort lookouts.

To counter this, Walker closed *Audacity* and requested that an aircraft be flown off at dawn to search for about twenty miles around the convoy. He vaguely hoped that in the grey half-light of a winter morning a surface U-boat might be caught unawares before it could submerge. He was lucky. Shortly after 9 am, when her fuel was running low, *Audacity*'s aircraft reported: U-BOAT ON SURFACE TWENTY-TWO MILES ON CONVOY'S PORT BEAM.

Ordering the destroyers *Exmoor*, *Blankney* and *Stanley*, and the corvette *Penstemon*, which was nearest to the aircraft's position, to join him, Walker turned *Stork* and set off at full speed. As the five ships raced away, the remainder of the escort closed the gaps by drawing nearer to the convoy. A lamp blinked GOOD HUNTING from the Commodore's ship leading the centre column of the convoy, and, after a cheerful thank you, Walker concentrated on meeting the enemy for the first time.

Blankney reached the position first and found a number of asdic echoes, two of which she classified as coming from a submarine, and proceeded to attack with depth-charges. When the rest arrived, Walker was unable to find anything remotely resembling a U-boat echo and, calming the exuberant *Blankney*, he formed the ships into line abreast for a sweep westwards, assuming that the submarine would continue on the convoy's course.

The slower *Penstemon*, plugging along in the rear, then picked up an echo. She reported the contact and Walker sent *Stanley* to assist her. He gave both ships instructions to rejoin him as soon as they lost contact — an order that was to prolong the battle for several hours. *Penstemon* attacked with a pattern of ten depth-charges and, after the boiling sea had simmered down, neither she nor *Stanley* was able to regain contact. In accordance with Walker's orders they left the area to rejoin with *Stork*.

By the time they caught up with the search party, Walker had asked *Audacity* to assist by flying off an aircraft to replace the one that had landed after making the original sighting report.

The hunt was developing into a full-scale offensive lunge, rarely employed by escort groups in those days. It was more usual to stay close to the convoy and wait for the U-boats to attack in the hope of keeping them at bay rather than set off in full chase, thereby leaving dangerous gaps in the screen. In fact, it was almost unheard of for an escort commander to take five of his ships on a hunt more than twenty miles from the convoy. Walker was by no means ignorant of his personal risk if a concerted attack were made on the convoy while he was away. To justify this hunt, he would have to make a kill.

The searching ships in line abreast and one mile apart were now well out on the port bow of the convoy with no sign of a contact. Walker decided to turn back and sweep eastwards across the front of the convoy. He had just sent the order when the ships on the extreme port side of the line signalled: OBJECT ON HORIZON TO STARBOARD.

Having spent the night jogging along behind the convoy, Baumann decided to take his boat up ahead for the next day. By his reckoning, there should be enough of his fellow-submariners in the vicinity for the attack to start after dusk. Keeping the convoy at visibility distance, he increased to full speed and had reached the port beam when, in the dawning overcast sky, he heard the sound of aircraft. As *U-131*'s alarm blared, a plane appeared from the cloud and swept low over her. Baumann and the conning-tower crew leapt for the hatchway and tumbled down into the control room. A few seconds later they were diving rapidly.

Despite faulty hydrophones, he altered course towards the convoy in the hope of avoiding any surface attack that might follow his discovery by the aircraft. Half an hour later, unable to hear the approach of *Penstemon* and *Stanley*, he was thrown to the deck by the blast of exploding depth-charges. When the tumult had subsided, the crew of *U-131*, stunned by the closeness of the attack, investigated the damage. In a few minutes, with lights gone, batteries spreading deadly chloride gas, and an ominous leak near the stern, Baumann knew he would have to surface.

To do so there would mean disaster. He needed to put at least fifteen miles between himself and his attackers before he could surface and escape at high speed. He took the U-boat down to 600 feet, ordered full submerged speed of five knots and sat down to wonder which would be the first to force them up — the gas, the running-down batteries or the leak astern.

He was, perhaps, fortunate to be granted two hours before he had to surface. When the hatch was opened and he rushed out to the conning-tower, there was nothing immediately in sight. A few minutes later a lookout shouted: 'Ships astern, Kapitan.' Baumann turned and saw five ships heading towards him no more than seven miles away.

He called down to the engineer. 'I want every bit of speed you can get. We are being chased by warships.'

A few minutes after *Stanley*'s report, the 'object' was identified as a U-boat and Walker flashed along the line: OPEN FIRE INDEPENDENTLY WHEN IN RANGE. Directors swung the gun turrets round on to the target, range-takers called out ranges and the leading ships, *Stork*, *Exmoor* and *Blankney*, prepared for the first barrage. Walker ordered the Martlet fighter from *Audacity* to attack in the hope that her machine guns might help to slow down the fast-moving enemy.

It was the chance young Sub-Lieutenant George Fletcher, RNVR, had been hoping would come his way ever since he had qualified as a Fleet Air Arm pilot and been sent to a convoy training base for duties in the Atlantic. He banked his plane, screamed over the convoy and spotted the U-boat — a tiny target on the heaving sea — right ahead. He put the Martlet into a dive. The conning-tower came into his sights and he could dimly see figures clustered round a gun. Then the tracers floated up at him and it was time to press a thumb down hard on the firing button. The fighter jerked as its guns flamed. Suddenly, the Perspex windscreen shattered and smoke filled the cockpit.

Below, the watchers in the five racing ships, with the corvette *Penstemon* plodding gamely in the rear, saw the fighter begin its dive, heard the urgent clatter of gunfire and were shocked to see smoke gushing from the cockpit. Silently, and dazed by the speed of events, they followed the plane down until it crashed in a cloud of spray almost alongside the U-boat.

With the range only slightly less than seven miles, *Stork*, *Blankney* and *Exmoor* commenced firing. Soon, *Stanley* joined in the barrage, *Penstemon* still being too far astern for her single gun mounting forward to have any effect. The barrage lasted for nearly twenty minutes, with shells plastering the area around *U-131* until *Stork*'s masthead lookout reported: 'Enemy abandoning ship, Sir. Looks as though she's been hit badly.'

The 'cease fire' was hoisted and, as the smoke cleared and the range closed rapidly, they could see figures leaping from the conning-tower into the sea. Before they could reach the scene, however, *U-131* pointed her nose to the sky and slid stern first below the waves. Damaged first by depth-charges and then holed eight times by the striking force guns, she was of no further use to Doenitz.

Exmoor and *Blankney* picked up her crew, all screaming and wailing in the water and looking not in the least like supermen. Walker was pleased, even though he looked grim when his whaler recovered Fletcher's bullet-ridden body kept afloat by the sodden life-jacket.

He sent a signal to the Admiralty and the Commander-in-Chief, Western Approaches, then formed up his ships and returned to the convoy by 5.30 pm, eight hours after the hunt had started. There would be few who could now criticize his lunge from the screen. There might, perhaps, be more opportunities to use the same offensive tactics, for a quick interrogation of prisoners had disclosed the presence of other U-boats at the convoy.

That same night the congratulations arrived. One came from Sir Percy Noble which said with customary brevity well done.

The first round in the battle to get HG76 through the U-boat cordon had gone to Walker. His novel tactics introduced into the Atlantic for the first time had not only succeeded, but had wiped away any doubts that any of his Group's captains might have had of a leader who, in the words of one officer left behind with the convoy during the hunt, was 'Haring about the ocean at the expense of the convoy'.

At daylight on the 18th, Walker read a short service over the flag-covered body of Sub-Lieutenant Fletcher and, as it was consigned to the sea, all escorts and ships of the convoy dipped their ensigns in salute. *Audacity* flew off her dawn patrol and the Commodore signalled to Walker.

> *Never mind the gathering storm. With the score at one for nil, the convoy is confident it is in good hands.*

CHAPTER 5: U-BOAT KILLER

Kapitanleutnant Heyda was worried about *U-131*. There had been no report from her throughout the day of the 17th and none all night. Having made contact with the convoy in *U-434* shortly after midnight he had decided that, in the absence of 'homing' reports from his colleague, he had better take over as shadower. He was on the surface about ten miles from the convoy at dawn on the 18th checking the positions of the nearest escorts before diving to give the crew a chance to clean up the boat and have breakfast in peace. Carrying out a similar check on the port beam of the convoy, *Stanley* sighted him from a range of about six miles, on her port quarter. She broke R/T silence to report to Walker and turned away at high speed to attack. *Exmoor*, *Blankney* and the sloop *Deptford*, all of whom were stationed within reasonable distance of the enemy, were ordered to join her, Walker's principal concern being for *Stanley*'s asdic which had been breaking down.

She closed the enemy at twenty-four knots, hoping to get near enough to drop depth-charges with a reasonable chance of success. But she was soon sighted by *U-434*, which crash-dived in seconds with *Stanley* still some three miles away. At a mile from the diving position, she saw oil bubbles blow to the surface and, reducing speed, began dropping single depth-charges in a square around the area.

Blankney arrived and, picking up an asdic echo, dropped a quick pattern of five depth-charges set to explode at 150 feet. When the disturbance had died away, she regained contact and acted as directing ship, passing the range and bearing to the asdic-less *Stanley* who went in to drop a pattern of fourteen charges set to 150 and 300 feet. While the spray was still falling, the irrepressible *Blankney* — always willing to attack anything and everything — raced in and dropped a ten-charge pattern in the same place.

Below the two ships, *U-434* was reeling under the shock. The charges, tumbling down, were causing damage faster than it could be repaired. The conning-tower hatch cover cracked and a steady stream of water poured down at Heyda's feet as he stood gripping the periscope column for support. The lights went out and the auxiliary system failed. Another rocking blast put the steering gear out of action. The finale came when the next pattern — *Blankney*'s for luck — detonated so close that the blast pressure of the water exploded one of their own torpedoes in the stern tubes. Panicking men shouted for'ard; the wounded in the stern screamed. Heyda glanced quickly at the depth gauge. It showed them sinking rapidly and out of control. White-faced, but calm, he ordered tanks to be blown and called the crew to prepare for surfacing.

Stanley and *Blankney* were preparing for another attack when *U-434* came to the surface less than a mile ahead with such a rush that she nearly leapt out of the water. Joyously, *Blankney* turned to ram at full speed but was too late. Shouting and wailing like their comrades in *U-131*, this crew jumped into the water. The last came up through the conning-tower as *U-434* rolled over and sank. The two destroyers, with the recently arrived *Exmoor*, picked up survivors and rejoined the convoy, and Walker was able to signal that a second U-boat had been sunk.

During the morning two Focke-Wulfs appeared low on the horizon and *Audacity* flew off two of her Martlets to engage them before they had a chance to send out too many details on their radios. When they came out of cloud ahead of the enemy, the guns of both aircraft unfortunately jammed after the initial bursts and the two enemy bombers scuttled off, one damaged slightly. After this Walker arranged with *Audacity*'s captain that aircraft should be flown off for routine patrols round the convoys at dusk and dawn each day. Any U-boats answering the summons of the Focke-Wulfs would receive a warm welcome by HG76 from the air and the sea.

Early in the afternoon, *Exmoor* and *Blankney*, who were based at Gibraltar and had barely enough fuel to make the return trip, parted company reluctantly. Before they left, *Blankney* signalled to Walker:

> Regret very much having to leave you when the spoils of war are still waiting to be plucked. Good luck, am proud to have sailed under your orders.

While on passage to Gibraltar, *Blankney* heard disquieting news from her forty-five prisoners. She signalled *Stork* immediately with a warning:

> Have learned from prisoners that position, course and speed of convoy are known to enemy together with name of aircraft-carrier.

In the late afternoon, *Audacity* flew off her dusk patrol too early and nothing was sighted. But, as darkness approached, *Penstemon*, on the convoy's port beam, broke R/T silence to report sighting a U-boat on the surface about ten miles to port. Walker ordered her to attack and told off another corvette, *Convolvulus*, to join her. They gave chase and the U-boat dived. As nightfall would cloak the convoy too soon for Walker to direct the chase, he ordered the two ships to remain hunting only so long as there seemed a chance of sinking the U-boat.

While *Convolvulus* was taking down his orders, the men on the bridge went rigid as her asdic loudspeaker picked up the approach of torpedo propellers.

'Hard a' starboard,' shouted her captain. 'Full ahead.'

Painfully and slowly the bows of the little ship began to swing as the noise from the loudspeaker sounded like the rushing of express trains. Suddenly a lookout shouted:

'Torpedoes to port, Sir.'

The captain rushed to the side of the bridge in time to see the wakes of two torpedoes about twenty feet away. It had been a very near miss.

After dark, the two ships lost contact with the submarine and rejoined the convoy.

For the next few hours peace came to HG76. On the starboard quarter, two miles from the end merchant ship of the starboard column, Walker zigzagged in *Stork*. The next ship to his left was *Stanley*, covering the rear of the convoy from a patrol two miles dead astern.

The weather was fine, only slightly overcast and with a pale moon shining bleakly through occasional breaks in the cloud. The sea was behaving much the same as it had throughout the voyage; short and choppy, with a swell big enough to roll a small ship round without being too uncomfortable. The wind was light and bitterly cold.

At 3.45 on the morning of the 19th, *Stanley* reported by R/T, *Submarine in sight*. In his excitement the reporting officer forgot to say where or on what bearing from the convoy.

U-574 had been the third U-boat to contact HG76 late on the 16th. Since then she had been staying close but doing nothing to give herself away. Her commander, Oberleutnant Gegnalbach, had watched the sinking of *U-131* through his periscope and, slightly sickened, had slunk away to the stern of the convoy. He stayed there throughout the 18th while *U-434* was being chased and destroyed, and eventually decided to make his attack that night. He surfaced and, increasing speed to catch up with the rear ships, got to within three miles when the moon came out for longer than usual to bathe the scene in a pale glow. He saw an escort on his port bow and, at the same time, *Stanley* made her report. While *Stanley* turned to attack, Gegnalbach gave a curt order.

'Stand by torpedoes.'

'Attacking.'

'FIRE.'

Walker raged on the bridge of *Stork*. He had almost lived there throughout the trip, retiring to his cabin only to shave and collapse wearily and fully-dressed for an hour or two on his bunk during the day. Even then he could not relax. As senior officer of the escort every signal affecting the convoy or any ship in the escort was sent to *Stork* and had to be dealt with during these precious moments.

He could not see *Stanley* in the dark — they were about six miles apart — and she had given him no idea of what directions he should steer to support her attack. Grabbing the R/T phone he shouted her code name and ordered: *Fire an illuminant to indicate your position*. If a shadower had contact with the convoy there was nothing much to give away.

He had just replaced the telephone when *Stanley* came on the air with another report: *Torpedoes passing from astern*.

As this was being given to Walker, one of his lookouts sighted *Stanley* who blinked her recognition signal with a shaded Aldis lamp.

'At the moment,' wrote Walker in his Diary later, 'when everything seemed to be sorting itself out at once and I had my glasses on her, she went up, literally, in a sheet of flame hundreds of feet high. She thought the torpedoes were passing her.'

It was a few minutes after 4 am when *Stanley* was torpedoed, and Walker for the first time ordered his 'Operation Buttercup' to deal with this night attack. Escorts turned outwards from the convoy firing starshell over the areas ordered by the 'Buttercup' instructions in an effort to illuminate the probable directions of the U-boat's escape on the surface. Walker took *Stork* close to the burning, sinking *Stanley* and dropped depth-charges in case the attacker had submerged and was trying to escape detection by hiding from asdics in the disturbance caused by the wreck. He took care not to go closer than half a mile to avoid injuring any of *Stanley*'s survivors.

While turning round the stern of *Stanley*, Walker gained contact with what his asdic team called a 'certain' submarine. He went in to attack, dropping a pattern of ten charges set to 50 and 150 feet. Then he ran out for half a mile to turn again in readiness for another attack. The second run-in had just started when the U-boat surfaced 200 yards ahead. *Stork* increased to full speed and steered a collision course. The ensuing chase, which lasted for eleven minutes, is told in Walker's Battle Report.

As I went in to ram he ran away from me and turned to port. I followed and I was surprised to find later that I had turned three complete circles, the U-boat turning continuously to port just inside *Stork*'s turning-circle at only two or three knots slower than me. I kept her illuminated with snowflakes and fired at him with the four-inch guns until they could not be sufficiently depressed. After this the guns' crews were reduced to fist shaking and roaring curses at an enemy who several times seemed to be a matter of feet away rather than yards.

A burst of 0.5 machine-gun fire was let off when these could bear, but the prettiest shooting was made by my First Lieutenant, Lieut G. T. S. Gray, DSC, RN, with a stripped Lewis gun from over the top of the bridge screen. He quickly reduced the conning-tower to a mortuary. No men were seen to leave the U-boat although they must have jumped some time judging from the position in which we found the survivors later.

Eventually, *Stork* managed to ram her quarry just before the conning-tower. *U-574* hung for a second on *Stork*'s stem before rolling off and scraping underneath her until reaching the stern where she was greeted by a pattern of depth-charges set at shallowest settings. These blew her to pieces and even rocked *Stork* dangerously.

Several Germans in the water were blown to bits by the depth-charges, and Walker did not expect any survivors when he steamed over to where some English-sounding shouts in the water indicated they might be some of the men from the stricken *Stanley*. They were Germans, and with *Samphire* helping, *Stork* picked them up. From the prisoners, he learned that his latest kill had been *U-574*. With five prisoners aboard, Walker proceeded to search for *Stanley*'s survivors with extra lookouts and the asdic team watching for signs of other U-boats.

There was little hope of anyone surviving the fire that had followed the torpedo explosion in *Stanley*, but cries from the water soon disclosed that twenty-five of them were swimming in a group. *Stork*'s boats pulled away and brought them aboard. One died later.

In the middle of this operation there was a dull explosion and a flash from the direction of the convoy. It was the SS *Ruckinge*, which managed to send out her name on the radio before the crew abandoned ship. Walker ordered *Samphire* to stay until she had picked up all survivors, and took *Stork* back to the convoy at full speed. On the way, he stopped to rescue from a lifeboat the master, chief engineer and twelve others of the *Ruckinge*. By this time it was clear that more than one U-boat had attacked the convoy, but it was now nearly 5.30 am and they could expect some respite.

On board *Stork* at this stage were three *Stanley* survivors, fourteen from *Ruckinge*, seven from *U-131* and six from *U-574*. Walker reported the night's events to C-in-C, Western Approaches and to the Admiralty.

To crown a night of flame and smoke, a signal marked URGENT from the Admiralty reached them as dawn was breaking on the 19th, saying that six U-boats appeared to be in the convoy's vicinity!

The Group felt the loss of *Stanley* deeply and there was a sense of sadness that one of the convoy had been sunk despite their efforts. But, in return, they had inflicted a hammer blow on the enemy. In three days, he had lost three ocean-going submarines and their crews. No escort before them could claim such toll for so small a loss.

Fortunately, the day proved quiet with only sparring skirmishes. Walker, with *Stork*'s bows crushed in and bent sideways by the force of her collision with *U-574*, had no wish to drive her too hard. He had also lost the use of his asdic set and was virtually powerless to attack anything submerged.

In the afternoon, a Focke-Wulf appeared to starboard with the obvious intention of establishing their position, course and speed for a night U-boat attack. Walker ordered *Audacity*'s aircraft up. 'The resulting battle was pretty to watch,' says his War Diary. 'The two Martlets climbed at the enemy alternately as he attempted to escape first in the clouds and then low over the sea. They presently returned, leaving a very dead Focke-Wulf.'

The carrier's dusk patrol sighted a U-boat on the surface fifteen miles away on the port beam, and immediately Walker ordered *Deptford*, *Marigold* and *Convolvulus* to hunt him at utmost speed, while he fumed at *Stork*'s own inability to join in the search because of her 'bent beak and my own stupidity in getting the dome[5] knocked off'. But the force returned after dark, having found nothing, only to be mistaken by some of the merchant ships for U-boats. The ensuing bout of pyrotechnics as they fired their snowflakes to illuminate the enemy did not, however, disturb the remainder of the night. The U-boats were around, but for some reason failed to press home the attack. Perhaps they had learned of the fate served out to their three colleagues.

The 20th passed uneventfully except for occasional darts outwards by *Audacity*'s aircraft to attack U-boats reported shadowing the convoy, and by noon on the 21st Walker had made up his mind that, no matter what evasive alterations of course it took, the convoy was still going to be shadowed. Therefore he might as well take the shortest route home. In his War Diary, he wrote with obvious weariness: 'The net of U-boats seems to be growing tighter around us despite *Audacity*'s heroic efforts to keep them at arm's length.'

That night, when the moon had gone behind a thick layer of overcast, he turned the convoy on to a course heading straight

---

[5] The asdic dome sticks out from the bottom of a ship like a small blister. It sends out the 'pings' which echo back when hitting an underwater obstacle.

for the Western Approaches while he continued with a small escort force on a northwesterly course, the convoy's general direction for the past few days. Once well away from the convoy, he staged a mock battle with the ships firing their starshell and snowflakes and dashing around as though in search of U-boats. Walker hoped that any U-boats shadowing them would be persuaded by the fuss that they had somehow lost the convoy and would come hurrying over to rejoin. In this way, he would draw them off HG76 and bring them to his doorstep where his 'feudin' and fussin'' force of decoys could get them on the surface.

Unfortunately, some merchantmen, seeing all this happen on the horizon, thought they were being attacked and immediately started firing their own snowflakes to warn their escort of an enemy attack and to see if a stray U-boat had penetrated into the convoy lanes. With the true position of the convoy now revealed — starkly, while the snowflake burned — and his ace-in-the-hole tipped off to the enemy, Walker took his force back to resume escort positions.

Stork had no sooner taken up her own station astern of the convoy when the balloon went up again. Still on his bridge, for the fourth day and night, Walker turned at a shout from his Officer of the Watch to see a ship disintegrate in flames on his starboard bow. Immediately, he called up the Group on R/T and ordered a 'Buttercup' illuminations search to starboard of the convoy. This was a blunder, which he later admitted. The torpedoed ship was, in fact, the last in the line of the centre column and the search should have been ordered astern of the convoy.

A few minutes later, about 11 pm, the carrier *Audacity*, which had done such noble work with her aircraft flying in impossible weather, reported herself torpedoed. Walker's Battle Report says:

> For the last three nights, *Audacity* with one corvette had zigzagged independently well clear of the convoy. Before dark tonight she had asked for a corvette and proposed to operate on the starboard side of the convoy. I had regretfully refused the corvette since I had only four escorts immediately around the convoy. I also suggested she should take station to port of the convoy since I anticipated any attack from the starboard side. *Audacity* replied that the convoy's alterations of course to port would inconvenience her and eventually she went off to starboard alone.
>
> I should have finally ordered her either on to the port side or into the middle of the convoy and I feel myself accordingly responsible for her loss.

Marigold, Convolvulus and *Samphire* were sent off to starboard where the carrier listed badly ten miles away. Of the survivors, one was in immaculate uniform, sitting in a Carley raft with a suitcase full of personal belongings. He was a young lieutenant, RNVR, who, the moment *Audacity* had parted with the convoy that evening to starboard, had announced to the wardroom: 'The senior officer of the escort is right, you know, chaps. We should have gone to port. And to back it up I'm going to pack my bags and put one in a raft all ready for the bright and jolly evacuation.' It had seemed quite a good joke a few hours before.

Walker had been in an awkward and, in many respects, unfair position. Although senior officer of the escort, and as such able to call on *Audacity* for assistance in hunting down the enemy, the commanding officer of the carrier, Commander D. W. MacKendrick, RN, was his senior.

Walker's job was to protect the convoy and see it through as intact as possible. *Audacity* was there to help him do it. On that last night, he felt the convoy needed the greater measure of protection and refused to part with a corvette to screen what he considered to be *Audacity*'s recklessness in manoeuvring to starboard of the convoy — the danger side. But in terms of seniority he could not give orders to MacKendrick on anything, and he was reluctant to argue openly by signal the niceties of rank between the senior officer of an escort and the commanding officer of an aircraft carrier.

It fell to *Penstemon* to sight Commander MacKendrick swimming among the oil and debris in a state of collapse. He was on their weather side and the ship was rolling heavily in mounting sea and swell. The ship's boat was away picking up other survivors and, when he saw the danger of the drowning officer being cut to ribbons by the keel, Lieutenant Williams, RNVR, the First Lieutenant, stripped off his jacket and plunged overboard to try and tie a rope round the exhausted Commander. MacKendrick's body, supported only by a life jacket, floated limply on the water. Williams managed to get a lifebuoy round him and signalled his crew to haul the officer on board. But while they were trying to pull him to the ship's side, a particularly heavy roll jerked the rope out of their hands. Members of the crew had just enough time to grab the exhausted Williams before MacKendrick drifted away in the swell. That was the last seen of him.

While the rescue work was going on, *Deptford*, on the convoy's port beam, sighted a U-boat on the surface between herself and the convoy. Walker joined her, firing starshell, and *Deptford* ran in to attack. The enemy dived and, for the next hour, *Deptford* and *Stork* carried out a series of depth-charge attacks until finally all contact was lost. In their opinion, the U-boat had sunk but, in the absence of any evidence, such as wreckage or survivors, Walker refused to confirm it as a 'kill'. They made several more runs on what appeared to be a submarine lying deep. Eventually, Walker called off the attack, classified it as a 'probable kill' and stationed *Deptford* on the convoy's port beam with *Stork* on the bow. This submarine was later admitted by the Germans to have been destroyed and was identified as another 740-tonner, *U-567*, commanded by Kapitanleutnant Endrass.[6]

By three in the morning of the 22nd, a lull in the fighting gave Walker a chance to assess the position. Once again, only one of the convoy had gone down, the Norwegian tanker, SS *Annavore* (3,000 tons), but the loss of *Audacity* with her aircraft was the most grievous blow. In retaliation they had beaten off most attacks and scored a 'probable'. Walker ordered the corvettes picking up survivors to return to the screen and on the bridge murmured aloud a prayer that the U-boats would spend the rest of the night licking their wounds and regrouping.

Fifteen minutes later, *Stork*'s crew were startled by an unusually heavy crash. Walker and the bridge personnel rushed to look aft and to their astonishment saw the bows of *Deptford* cutting into *Stork*'s quarterdeck. A lookout in *Deptford* had seen what he thought was a U-boat close on the surface. The Officer of the Watch had altered course and crammed on full speed, at the same time calling his captain who was down in the chartroom estimating the convoy's position. When it was too late, the 'U-boat' was seen to be *Stork*.

Damage was serious if not vital. Describing the scene in his War Diary, Walker wrote: '*Deptford*'s stem had walked straight

---

[6] Endrass had been First Lieutenant of *U-47*, commanded by Gunter Prien, when she penetrated Scapa Flow earlier in the war.

into the temporary prison and two of the five Boche captives there were pulped literally into a bloody mess. When I went aft in the dark later to inspect the damage I walked straight into the hole and found myself with my feet among the Boche corpses and my elbows on the quarterdeck.'

When he had been helped back on deck, he turned to a group of sailors and muttered quietly: 'Well, well, well. Never a dull moment.' Then he returned to the bridge.

There were no further attacks that night, but at dawn on the 22nd, the balance sheet showed a gloomy picture — as far as the escort was concerned. *Stork*'s asdic equipment was useless; her depth-charges had to be moved to the bows to lighten the stern damaged by *Deptford*; and her speed had been reduced to ten knots; *Deptford* herself had a damaged stern, her asdic was out of action and her maximum speed was eleven knots; most of the Group's radar sets had packed up; *Audacity* and her aircraft had followed *Stanley* to the bottom.

During the day, a Liberator arrived to patrol round the convoy for nearly three hours. At this time a Focke-Wulf paid them a brief visit but soon vanished in the clouds. At 4 pm, as darkness was falling, the Liberator reported two U-boats on the surface twenty-five miles astern of the convoy.

They were lying alongside each other, when the aircraft broke cloud, and a wide plank bridged the gap between them. Men were crossing from one to another and it seemed likely they were repairing some sort of damage. The aircraft dived and shot three men off the plank before the U-boats drew apart. It was learned later that one of them had been holed previously either by depth-charges or gunfire during the convoy battle and had been trying to repair damage that prevented her diving. When the aircraft appeared, the crew of the damaged U-boat transferred to the other, leaving behind scuttling charges. When the latter left the scene at high speed on the surface and the other one sank as the scuttling charges went off, the aircraft thought she had submerged.

The U-boat had quite certainly been damaged by the escort and finished off unwittingly by the aircraft. The score could now read four and a half U-boats destroyed by the Group, as they shared honours with the Liberator for this last kill.

At midnight, the SS *Ogmore Castle* shuddered under a particularly heavy sea. Officers and crew were suddenly convinced that they had rammed a U-boat, and were holed themselves. They rushed to the boats and abandoned ship. *Convolvulus* investigated, found the deserted ship to be floating quite serenely and informed the crew in the lifeboats that they could re-board their ship. By dawn, the *Ogmore Castle* had resumed her station in the convoy, manned by a sheepish crew.

The night passed without further incident — the quietest for seven days — and, at noon on the 23rd, the convoy was led into the Western Approaches 'safe' area by an exhausted but happy Group.

The Commodore signalled Walker: *Despite the loss of* Audacity *and* Stanley, *you have won a great victory. On behalf of the convoy deepest congratulations and many thanks.* Walker acknowledged and set off for Plymouth to have *Stork*'s damaged 'beak' repaired. The convoy that had to get through had started off from Gibraltar with thirty-two ships and now arrived in the United Kingdom thirteen days later with two fewer.

Before docking in Plymouth, Walker received a message from Sir Percy Noble saying:

> You are required to attend a meeting with myself and the Director of Anti-Submarine Warfare at the Admiralty at 1500 on Tuesday, January 6th,

CHAPTER 6: 'SPLICE THE MAINBRACE'

Ashore in Plymouth, Walker telephoned his wife and arranged to meet her in London. He held a series of conferences with his First Lieutenant and the Dockyard Superintendent to facilitate the effective and speedy repair of *Stork-*, sent his Report of Proceedings of the last voyage to the Admiralty; and eventually vanished from Plymouth for a week's rest.

In the days that followed, the Admiralty issued a statement announcing the award of the DSO, but to Walker the Press publicity was not only unexpected, but unwanted. He cringed from the thought of his name being published in anything more widely read than the Navy List. When a staff officer phoned to say the naval reporters wished to interview him, he instructed that his whereabouts be kept secret. For the remainder of his leave he was nervous if the telephone rang or anyone other than a tradesman called at his house.

According to his elder sister, now Mrs Georgina Forbes, he had once appeared as a child ballet dancer before a huge audience at the Albert Hall which had led to a fit of uncontrollable sobbing and a hatred of ever again making a spectacle of himself. It may be that his passionate dislike of publicity stemmed from this experience.

Now, as an active service commander, although still subconsciously frightened of making a spectacle of himself, he resented any invasion of his privacy and was forever indignant that any individual should be singled out for public acclaim when the work had been done by a team.

At 3 pm on January 6th, he entered the office of the Director of Anti-Submarine Warfare at the Admiralty to find Admiral Sir Percy Noble, Captain George Creasy and other senior officers already in conference and waiting for him. Despite his commanding height and lean, tanned appearance, he shrank from talking too freely in front of superiors and subsided into his chair in the hope that his presence might be forgotten. But he had been invited specially to give the conference a chance to discuss the strategic and tactical policy of the U-boat war in the light of his experience with HG76.

He answered questions briefly, saying much in few words. His impact on the Atlantic battle had been sudden and successful and, through the reports of Sir Percy Noble and Captain Creasy, more swiftly recognized by the Admiralty than was usual in that citadel of conservatism. When question time was over, he was asked to make recommendations for future operations. This was unexpected, but he gave his reply without pulling punches.

(1) Aircraft are absolutely invaluable for anti-submarine work. There should be shore-based patrol planes for hunting down U-boats and carrier-borne fighters for destroying the Focke-Wulf bombers on 'homing' patrols. *Audacity*, her staff and pilots, put up a matchless performance.

(2) Every effort should be made to provide convoys with two protective screens — an outer and an inner. By day the outer screen sights U-boats on the surface farther away from the convoy and can attack in offensive striking forces well clear of the merchantmen. By night, U-boats are forced to attack from between the screens or at least to penetrate both.

(3) By day, all escorts should be used as striking forces for offensive lunges away from the convoy, attacking U-boats detected as far away as thirty miles.

(4) The 36th Escort Group 'Operation Buttercup' is a second plan despite my putting it into operation on the wrong side on one occasion. But snowflake illuminant rockets are a menace in the convoy. I am well aware that merchant ships are fitted with this to 'turn night into day'. But I feel strongly that there should be no guarantee that snowflakes will not be fired at exactly the wrong moment. Neither can we legislate for the regrettable tendency of some ships in an emergency, real or imaginary, to fire everything, drop everything and abandon ship.

It was his third point that brought immediate opposition. His remarks on air cooperation were to be passed to Coastal Command; the question of ships for outer and inner screen, although desirable for the future, was dismissed as impracticable at the present moment due to lack of available ships; and his comment on snowflakes in merchant ships was brushed aside as being based on an isolated and unfortunate experience.

The question of whether escorts should be used as striking forces for forays against the enemy well away from the convoy aroused instant opposition.

Privately, Walker determined to go his own way and rely on success to keep him out of trouble. By the time he left the room he had no doubts that he would be a watched man. When his leave was up, he returned to Plymouth while Eilleen stayed on in London. With her husband and two sons in uniform — Timmy was serving in a destroyer and Nicholas a sub-lieutenant in *Ajax* — she had decided to take a war job herself and was about to start in the Naval Section of Censorship.

Walker found in Plymouth that *Stork* would not be ready until March, but on January 10th he was ordered to take temporary command of a sloop, *Pelican*, and lead his Group to sea for another trip to Gibraltar. Before sailing he called on board *Stork* and found waiting for him the official signals concerning his decoration.

To his officers, who would stay with *Stork* while she was being repaired and Walker went to sea in *Pelican*, he seemed somewhat overwhelmed by the honour which had come his way so unexpectedly; and to their affectionate amusement was obviously very shy about the whole thing.

The Group, consisting of *Samphire*, *Rhododendron*, *Penstemon*, *Vetch*, *Marigold* and *Gardenia*, met *Pelican* off the Irish coast and rendezvoused with the convoy, CG78, in the approaches, northwest of Ireland. *Deptford* and *Convolvulus* remained behind in Liverpool for minor repairs.

For the next three days they battled southwards against a fierce, southerly gale, sheets of rain blotting out the horizon, the wind shrieking through the rigging and angry seas buffeting their bows. *Penstemon* reported all her lifeboats smashed and most of the Group had suffered damage to vital equipment. By the 16th the convoy had been scattered and only thirteen of the original twenty-six ships were in sight. Three more sleepless nights were spent in rounding up the lost ones and, at dawn on the 19th, it looked as though most of the flock had been returned to the fold. But a rapid count showed eight still missing and the Group steamed off again into the boiling seas for another search.

Eventually, on the 21st, the weather abated and the risk of attack returned with calmer days. The Group took up their screen with four ships still unaccounted. No attack developed and, on the 24th, the convoy was delivered to Gibraltar intact except for the errant quartet who luckily survived all hazards and reached the Rock next day.

Three days later, they sailed again with a homeward-bound convoy, a trip remembered by the Group only for the exercises Walker ordered to increase 'team' efficiency. At any time of day he might order a variety of dummy attacks; at night, he would instruct all ships to carry out depth-charge drill and it was not considered safe for a commander to report progress until he could say his charges were ready within thirty seconds. By the time they reached the Western Approaches, most of the ships' companies were praying earnestly for a U-boat 'pack' to arrive and spare them all these fake alarms and scares.

On landing at Liverpool, Walker learned that *Stork* was to be ready for sea ahead of schedule and, after turning over *Pelican* to a new commanding officer, he entrained for Plymouth to take his own ship to sea again. The next day, slim dapper young Sub-Lieutenant John Filleul, RN, arrived in Plymouth to join *Stork*. After nine years in Canada, he had followed his father into the Navy; but for a number of reasons — probably caused by recent Canadian influence on his outlook — he had felt rather a misfit in his last ship, a cruiser in which pomp was expected and frequent parades. As he boarded *Stork* he was filled with misgivings about the future. Perhaps this was another ship in which all he did would bring down the wrath of both captain and first lieutenant.

He was standing on the quarterdeck idly watching an officer cross the gangway and vanish below when a voice shouted:

'Who was that who just came aboard, Sub?'

Filleul turned to face the First Lieutenant and muttered that he did not know. Secretly he wondered how he, a newcomer, could reasonably be expected to know. Later, a tall, athletic-looking commander came aboard, glanced at Filleul and said:

'Come down to my cabin, Sub.'

Filleul groaned inwardly. What had he done wrong already? From experience he knew that interviews with commanders could be unpleasant milestones in a young officer's life. Instead, the senior officer introduced himself as Commander Walker and invited him to have a gin.

From that moment, the young Sub-Lieutenant viewed senior officers in a different light; his bias against the Service fell away and, like all other officers who served under Walker in the years ahead, it was the beginning of a discipleship, almost a dedication, to a captain he admired and respected above all others.

Walker spent the next trip working up his own ship's company after their long spell in harbour and resumed exercising the Group — often to the amusement of the convoy Commodore who interrupted intricate manoeuvres with a stream of rude signals. Walker retaliated by 'requesting' the Commodore to exercise his convoy in a variety of evasive turns, so that 'I can keep my escort up to scratch and assist in the working out of new escort stations'. It was a flimsy enough excuse but served to give the by now thoroughly irate Commodore some anxious moments as the lumbering merchantmen either failed to see his altering course signals or merely decided to ignore them.

This flock also arrived at the Rock without incident and, almost immediately, the Group about-turned to bring HG80 home to England — a convoy the enemy refused to attack.

While lying in Gladstone Dock waiting to be ammunitioned and stored for the next voyage, *Stork* was inspected by Admiral Sir Percy Noble. Walker laid on a special display of action drills and afterwards the ship's company were mustered on the quarterdeck to be addressed by their Commander-in-Chief.

'I am very much impressed,' said Sir Percy, 'with the efficiency of this ship. We can win this battle against the U-boats only by constant drilling and training — and you are all well drilled and well trained. You have been successful in your actions against the enemy and it would take a blind man to fail to see your keenness and eagerness to come to grips with him again. I am proud of you all.'

Later, in the privacy of his office, Sir Percy told his Chief of Staff:

'That crowd in *Stork* are an amazingly efficient team. They can run and fight their ship blindfold. And every one of them adores Walker. I could see they would follow him without question anywhere he chose to lead. If we can get all our ships trained and keyed up to that pitch we will make the U-boat crews wish they had never been born.'

When the 36th Group sailed again from Liverpool on April 12th, Walker was becoming a little concerned about his ships. So many trips with only drills and exercises to relieve the strain and tension of guarding against attacks which never materialized, made him suspect that his commanding officers were getting stale. He hoped sincerely that the enemy would soon make some sort of an appearance.

As if the enemy were reading his mind, he received on the 14th a warning from the Admiralty that a U-boat was in the vicinity of his convoy — HG82 — probably about thirty miles away. That evening Walker had taken *Stork* to the stern of the convoy — the most dangerous position, as U-boats were known to be fond of night attacks from the stern — and *Vetch* was in station about two miles ahead of the convoy's port column. At 9.30 *Vetch*'s radar operator reported an object about four miles on the port quarter; this would put it about three miles on the port bow of the column's leading ship. *Vetch* turned hurriedly to investigate and approached what at first sight appeared to be a corvette end-on, which she took to be her sister ship, *Penstemon*.

Her commanding officer, however, had thoroughly absorbed the teachings, drills and exercises of his Group leader, and, leaving nothing to chance, fired a round of starshell to make sure. In the pale glare of the shell, they saw a U-boat, *U-252*, less than a mile away, and heading fast into the convoy. At once, they saw it wheel round; then the bridge watch heard the unmistakable sounds of torpedoes approaching on the asdic loudspeaker. *Vetch* took drastic evasive action while breaking R/T silence to tell Walker: *Submarine one mile away from us.*

The torpedoes missed *Vetch* by about twenty feet and she opened fire just as the U-boat decided to dive. Her next report to *Walker* — *Submarine has dived* — caused some agitation in *Stork*, for again it gave no position or indication that *Vetch* had left her station ahead of the port column. However, Walker saw *Vetch*'s machine-gun tracer bullets and, heading towards them at full speed, ordered the corvette to indicate her position by firing a snowflake rocket. As soon as this had been done and the area of the attack pinpointed to the port side of the convoy, he altered course to join *Vetch* and instructed the remainder of the Group to stay close to the convoy. By the time he arrived, the convoy had drawn ahead and *Vetch* was searching for asdic contact.

Just as *Stork* was coming abreast of *Vetch*, the U-boat surfaced ahead of them about a mile away, and both ships gave chase. The enemy proved an elusive target and *Stork* herself fired more than a hundred rounds without any hits being observed. This was no reflection on the gunnery, but rather a measure of what a small target is presented to the firing ship by a 500-ton U-boat trimmed down on the surface on a dark night and at a fine, slanting inclination to the hunter.

Vetch, a little overwhelmed at the drama of the chase and the presence of Walker, excitedly broke R/T silence to claim four hits. Walker remained unimpressed and his doubts were justified at 10.30 pm when the U-boat suddenly crash-dived — an unlikely procedure had it been hit and holed.

Vetch was nearest the diving point and, anticipating orders, ran in to drop a ten-charge pattern in the still swirling water. As she drew clear, Walker took *Stork* in for a second attack with ten more charges set to explode rather deeper. Between them the two ships carried out five attacks, dropping fifty depth-charges in the next twenty minutes and, at 11 pm, Walker called off *Vetch* and waited for something to appear. He wrote in his Diary:

> I was tolerably certain that the Boche had been poleaxed — as indeed he had. Wreckage boiled to the surface and in high daylight I had a boat lowered to investigate.

As they steamed back to the convoy *Vetch* signalled Walker requesting permission to splice the mainbrace. In his reply, Walker said: *Approved and heartiest congratulations on your excellent work.* To which the elated little corvette commented: *Very Many Thanks. Let's have another one.*

Shortly after midnight, both ships received signals from the First Sea Lord and C-in-C, WA, saying *Well Done.*

Vetch's signal set the pattern for celebrating all Walker's future successes. From then on, it became customary for all ships under his command to 'splice the mainbrace' after every confirmed kill.

Two days later they sighted a merchant ship's Carley raft bobbing forlornly out to starboard. Walker took *Stork* close, and it seemed to be empty; certainly no one was getting excited about the approach of a warship. Suddenly a lookout shouted:

'There's a dog still alive, Sir.'

Sure enough, when they came alongside there was a small, grey-brown mongrel of obscure parentage huddled in a corner of the raft, too wet and weak to raise more than a whimper.

A few minutes later he was aboard *Stork* being warmed, fed and cared for as no waif drifting about the Atlantic had ever been cared for before — indeed it is unlikely that a puppy has ever been found in such circumstances. In no time he was called 'Buster' and, when capable of sounding off a few healthy yaps, trotted off to inspect the ship. He found it a 'likely craft' and showed his democratic spirit by making a daily visit to both wardroom and mess decks. After several trips, the thunder of roaring depth-charges left him as unmoved as the crack of the guns. He adopted an action station on the bridge, despite the almost vertical ladders he had to climb unaided. Normally, he would sit around waiting to be carried up or down, but the moment the alarm bells rang he took the ladders in his stride under his own steam.

Nothing further interfered with the peaceful passage of the convoy, which arrived at Gibraltar intact on the 24th.

The sinking of *U-252* had all the ingredients of a classic Walker attack. With a minimum of signalling, the Group was split into two units — the hunting team and the continuing escort with the convoy. During the action, the value of drills emerged as an essential to success. The depth-charge crews, the asdic team, the guns' crews and signalmen played split-second and vital roles. A hitch anywhere and a determined, clever and slippery opponent might have escaped to sink more ships on another day.

Throughout the attack the signalling of orders and report between *Vetch* and *Stork* were kept down to a total of eight messages, embracing twenty-five words.

The final chapter in the U-boat's life was told by Walker who, as usual, played down his own share.

'*Vetch* acted with exemplary initiative and dash,' he wrote. 'He saved the convoy from attack, and his bulldog tenacity in clinging on to the U-boat was mainly responsible for bringing her to a very fitting end. To him must be given the larger slice of credit. No doubt she received a blow from *Stork* just where the chicken got the axe, but it was *Vetch*'s final pattern which doubtless reduced all buoyant remains of the U-boat and crew to the disgusting mess of junk, matchwood and butcher's exhibits which were later found.' Among the awards was the first Bar to Johnnie Walker's DSO.

Two more voyages across the Bay of Biscay passed without more than irritating skirmishes with the enemy which kept the Group in a constant state of readiness. They returned to Gibraltar in May and, on June 9th, sailed again to rendezvous with HG84 for the trip home. Wear, tear and enemy action had reduced the 36th Escort Group to *Stork*, *Marigold*, *Convolvulus* and *Gardenia*, *Vetch* stayed in Gibraltar for repairs.

The Group's career had been short, eventful and successful. Whenever the enemy had approached in number they had been counter-attacked until forced to retire while the Group sailed home with trophies and prisoners. In between they had their full share of patient, monotonous slogging, waiting for an enemy who rarely appeared but might easily launch surprise attacks at the most unlikely times. This had taken its toll of the Group's strength and they needed action to restore morale.

The four ships of the decimated 36th Escort Group took over

convoy HG84 off Gibraltar on June 9th. It consisted of twenty merchantmen, with Commodore H. T. Hudson, RNR, sailing in the SS *Pelano*, leading ship of the centre column. In the port outer column was a CAM ship,[7] *Empire Morn*, while astern of the convoy was the SS *Copeland*, the rescue ship responsible for picking up survivors should any of the convoy be sunk. She was equipped with up-to-date medical instruments and her decks were laid out like a hospital ward. Survivors could look forward to every comfort in *Copeland*, providing she herself did not get torpedoed.

Walker stationed his escorts about the convoy in accordance with his usual practice — although four ships could hardly be called a screen. By day, he patrolled ahead of the convoy with *Marigold* on starboard beam, *Gardenia* to port and *Convolvulus* astern. At night he changed places with *Convolvulus*, taking *Stork* to the stern, the position from which a shadower might be intercepted.

To the convoy, the sight of a lone sloop with three ponderous corvettes in attendance could not have presented too comforting a sight or provided an uplift for men about to cross the most dangerous strip of water in the entire Atlantic battlefield — the Bay of Biscay. At the convoy conference held on the Rock before sailing, the briefing officer had been subjected to some grim sarcasm when he told the Merchant Navy captains the size of their escort.

Walker headed northwards to a rendezvous with three more ships due to join the convoy from Lisbon. These arrived on the 12th and the convoy settled down on a northerly course, certain now of attack, for the newcomers had been shadowed to the main convoy by a Focke-Wulf. Already their position, with probable course and speed, would be plotted on the

---

[7] These were known as Catapult Aircraft Merchantmen.

charts of every U-boat within hearing distance of the aircraft's signals. Walker nearly ordered the *Empire Morn*'s fighter up to shoot down the intruder, but this was a trick that could only be pulled once and he decided to save it for another and possibly more urgent occasion. In any event, the weather might not have been calm enough to ensure the safe recovery of the pilot. The sea was running fairly rough in a high wind and the swell was long enough to start several of the convoy swinging dangerously close to each other.

During the 13th, enemy aircraft were never far away, appearing at intervals in gaps between the low-lying, fast-moving cloud which provided excellent cover for their patrols. Next day, the Focke-Wulfs kept up their shadowing activities in relays until Walker decided that they might be more cautious and less eager if one or more could be destroyed. He ordered *Empire Morn* to fly off her Hurricane to shoot down the one Focke-Wulf in sight and to patrol until fuel ran out and the pilot was forced to ditch. The fighter was catapulted into the air shortly after noon and soared off to engage the enemy. Unfortunately, the pilot managed to get only two quick bursts at the shadower before he found a cloud and vanished into its cover. An hour later he pancaked neatly alongside a ship in the starboard column and was picked up as the plane broke in the sea.

At 4 pm the rescue ship, *Copeland*, intercepted on HF/DF[8] a U-boat signalling its first sighting report of the convoy from somewhere in the outfield on the port quarter of the convoy. Walker had to choose — to keep his slender screen intact round the convoy, or to dart out to attack the chattering U-boat. Most captains at that time would have taken the safer, and in many ways the sounder, course of staying with the

---

[8] An instrument for intercepting U-boat wireless signals.

convoy in the hope of beating off the 'pack', but Walker, restless and impatient to destroy the enemy before he could attack the convoy, signalled *Gardenia* to join *Stork*, and raced away to hunt down the homing U-boat. By taking this decision he virtually threw away the rule book and staked his career on the success of the offensive lunge and his belief that the convoy would be quite safe in the hands of *Convolvulus* and *Marigold* during his absence.

The two ships steamed for nearly fifty minutes at 15 knots, *Gardenia*'s maximum speed, before a lookout in *Stork*'s crow's nest shouted excitedly down the voice pipe to the bridge:

'Submarine on the surface dead ahead, Sir.'

They had been lucky to sight the target so quickly. While this information was being flashed to *Gardenia*, Walker ordered full speed and sent for his engineer officer. Only a brief glance at the conning-tower dimly visible in the haze ten miles away was needed for him to rush back to the engine-room to begin coaxing the last revolution possible from the straining, willing engines.

Almost at once they were sighted by the enemy, who turned rapidly and began running away on the surface, evidently hoping she could out-distance her hunters. In fact, she was a knot or two slower than *Stork*, whose crew, closed up at action stations, were already training their guns on the target. But they were still out of range. At seven miles they could hope to reach him; at six and a half they could probably score hits.

Two hours later, *Gardenia* was dropping farther and farther astern and, in *Stork*, the range-finder crew were calling out the ranges as the gap narrowed with painful slowness.

'Fourteen thousand five hundred, Sir.'[9]

They were overhauling steadily.

---

[9] One nautical mile is equivalent to 2,000 yards.

'Fourteen thousand, Sir.'

A minute had passed, seeming like an hour.

'Thirteen thousand six hundred, Sir.'

The guns' crews tensed for the order to open fire, when suddenly the U-boat decided he could not outstrip the sloop and crash-dived. As it vanished in a faintly discernible swirl of bubbling water, Walker was presented with a nasty theoretical problem. It would take *Stork* nearly twenty minutes to reach the diving point and, in that time, the quarry could steam for about two miles at least in any direction. In seconds, Walker had to decide the direction he must steer to intercept and pick her up on the asdic.

The U-boat had dived on a northwesterly course. Logically, she might be expected to continue on that course to keep pace with the convoy and resume her shadowing should her attackers give up the chase. After signalling *Gardenia* to follow suit, Walker altered course slightly to the south, decreased speed and ordered his asdic team to commence their sweep. He had gambled on the enemy doing exactly the opposite to what might be expected. If the gamble failed and the U-boat slipped past them, the convoy would be at his mercy, virtually unprotected. There was another move. The U-boat Commander could torpedo his tormentor and rid himself of the fastest and most effective escort in the screen.

In the minutes that followed, the tension throughout *Stork* increased visibly as guns' crews, cheated of a target, moved to their platform rails with eyes searching for a periscope. On the bridge, Walker sat hunched in a wooden seat specially built for him behind the gyro compass. With a slight smile he murmured orders to the helmsman and kept one ear on reports from the asdic team.

Suddenly, the hoped-for report rang out.

'Echo bearing 340 degrees, Sir.'

The gamble had come off. He had intercepted the U-boat, thirty minutes after its dive. It was slightly on his starboard bow. The smile became a grin as he gave the order: 'Going in to attack.'

Stork shuddered under light helm and increased speed. The asdic operator shouted out the decreasing ranges as they ran towards the echo. The U-boat passed beneath.

'Fire …'

The asdic officer pressed the bell to the depth-charge crews in the stern, and ten charges of high explosive were shot into the air and tumbled from racks into the water. For nearly a minute the crew of *Stork* waited silently as she slowed down and turned. Then the ear-splitting cracks of detonating depth-charges roared in their ears and the boiling surging water was flung skywards. *Stork* altered course and the men leaned over at their action stations for signs of destruction. Not a pint of oil marked the position of the recent explosions. Their first attack had failed.

It took four more attacks to convince Walker that he had met a cunning opponent, not to be easily panicked into some desperate manoeuvre that would give him away. It seemed that he was varying his depth after every attack and probably circling at the same time inside *Stork*'s own turning circle. By this time, *Gardenia* had arrived, and Walker, his own supply of depth-charges reduced to eighteen, sent her in for a sixth attack.

One of *Gardenia*'s first ten depth-charges exploded prematurely and spectacularly, blowing her ensign into tatters and seriously damaging her stern and engine-room. She might still attack but would be ruled out as an efficient escort in future operations with the convoy.

The two ships kept up the hunt until 10 pm with *Stork* directing *Gardenia*'s attacks. As nightfall was approaching and the convoy drawing farther away, Walker decided to return before the 'pack' could launch its attack. He ordered *Gardenia* to continue with the hunt for as long as she was able, or until the U-boat had been destroyed, and himself set course to catch up the convoy at full speed.

On the other side of the convoy, *Marigold* was also hurrying to reach the convoy before dark. As Walker gained asdic contact with his U-boat, *Marigold* had left the convoy at high speed to hunt another reported fifteen miles away on the starboard bow. Her commanding officer had anticipated that this was what Walker would have wanted him to do and judged that, as the U-boats were not likely to attack until dark, *Convolvulus* could remain in sole possession of the field immediately round the convoy. *Convolvulus* did not protest, and an hour later *Marigold* sighted her quarry about to dive twelve miles away. She attacked a 'certain sub echo' three times before breaking off the action to resume her position on the screen. She expected to rejoin at about 1 am.

Walker arrived at the convoy at midnight and confidently took up his station astern. A quick analysis of the situation showed that the prospects for the night could have been worse; one U-boat was being kept down forty-five miles away on the port quarter by *Gardenia*; another, now thirty miles away, had been severely shaken by *Marigold*; *Convolvulus* had sneaked in a quick lunge during *Marigold*'s absence and chased a U-boat out of sight on the starboard bow; and if *Marigold* could resume her station by 1 am only *Gardenia* would be missing from the screen.

Marigold was fifteen minutes late rejoining, and in that vital time gap an undetected 'pack' pounced.

The Commodore's ship, *Pelavo*, was the first to go up. She vanished in a cloud of smoke, flame and spray, the blast of the exploding torpedo blowing Commodore Hudson through the canvas awnings over his bridge into the night. He was never seen again. Well astern of the convoy, the flash and roar of the torpedo striking home had just been reported in *Stork* and alarm bells were ringing when another ship, the SS *Strib*, was silhouetted starkly for a fraction of a second as two torpedoes struck her amidships. A third ship burst into flame on the other side of the convoy, the SS *Slendal*. All three sank in a few minutes.

Walker ordered his illuminant operation, 'Buttercup', to be put into effect astern of the convoy, unhappily aware that only his ship and *Marigold*, now coming up from astern, could hope to carry it out. It was a fruitless search. In fact, the attacking U-boats had come in on the bows and were retreating on the surface ahead of the convoy, successfully dodging the twisting and turning *Convolvulus*. Walker ordered *Marigold* to stay astern and assist *Copeland* to search for and rescue survivors. This was an unfortunate move. The U-boats had not yet finished with convoy HG84 for the night and were forming up for the second attack off the starboard beam, where *Marigold* would have been had she resumed her station.

There was a preliminary skirmish at 4 am when one of *Stork*'s lookouts sighted the wake of a U-boat just diving. Walker altered course towards it, increased to full speed and attacked with a pattern of ten charges. They exploded so accurately that he turned to his First Lieutenant on the bridge and announced with a triumphant grin: 'I shall be exceedingly surprised if history does not show that chap to have been well and truly sunk.' He was right but, suppressing a strong desire to linger and collect evidence, raced back to catch up with the stern of the convoy and resume his position.

At 4.30 am the U-boats struck back. The SS *Thurso*, in the middle of the convoy, literally exploded into fragments and for a moment seemed to disintegrate into a white, blazing ball of fire. Darkness had barely time to close in tightly again before the SS *City of Oxford* shuddered to a standstill under the impact of an internal explosion caused when the torpedo pierced her hull and detonated inside a cargo hold. She sank while the ships following her were altering course round her heavily listing hulk.

The chaos became complete when every ship in the convoy began firing snowflake illuminant rockets wildly and indiscriminately, lighting up every column until it became possible for an attacker to take his time about selecting a target. Walker was raging inwardly, and he almost danced in consternation when one of the ships astern opened fire with her machineguns, sending streams of tracers in a wide arc behind her, nearly hitting *Stork*'s bridge and moving round to spray the decks of her neighbouring ship in the next column. The latter, thinking he was under attack from the air, fired off everything he had at the nearest star.

It was all a bit too much for the escort and, under Walker's orders, they steamed at full speed round the convoy just outside the glare of the snowflakes in the hope of catching a U-boat stalking them on the surface.

When the convoy, now without a commodore until the vice-commodore could assume control, had decided to stop firing snowflakes, Walker ordered *Convulvulus* back to her station ahead and told off *Marigold* to continue assisting *Copeland* in her search for fresh survivors. What was left of the night passed quietly.

Walker felt deeply that he might have prevented the second attack if he had left *Marigold* to take up her normal position in the screen.

'I know that rescue work was the proper duty for *Copeland*,' he wrote later, 'but I am still uncertain if I was right or wrong in telling *Marigold* to help her. For because of this, *Marigold* was not in her position on the screen at 4.30 am when the second attack came from the starboard beam where she would have been. She would almost certainly have picked up the attackers on her radar. On the other hand *Copeland* would take a long time to pick up the survivors herself and would have fallen so far astern of the convoy that it is likely she would have been sunk.'

Crouched in his seat on the bridge, muffled in scarves and sweaters, he sat silent while the Officer of the Watch handled the ship. Daylight came and it was 8 am before he sat up, mumbled a few orders and went below to bathe, shave and eat a frugal breakfast.

He re-appeared on the bridge, refreshed. *Marigold* was crammed with survivors and, if she were to become a fighting unit again, they would have to be transferred to *Copeland* and his own ship. He sent the necessary signals and the three ships dropped astern of the convoy while the tiny corvette transferred 172 survivors. Walker grinned as he called over the loudhailer asking *Marigold* how she had stayed afloat. He was told: 'It would hardly appear seemly before our Merchant Navy friends for the rescue ship to be inhospitable, so we prayed.'

Stork had taken aboard her share, and more were in the process of boarding *Copeland*, when *Marigold* sighted a conning-tower six miles from her and ten miles from the convoy. Despite the indignant protests of the few survivors still waiting to be transferred, the corvette jumped through the water in pursuit of the enemy. The U-boat, sighting the corvette leaping over the choppy seas towards her, turned and ran off, showing *Marigold* a fast-vanishing stern. The corvette about-turned, rejoined *Copeland* and sent across her last survivors.

In the evening, *Gardenia* appeared on the horizon and her signal lamp blinked a cautious claim: *Consider I finished him off*.

At dawn, Walker sent a signal to the Commander-in-Chief, Western Approaches, informing him of the night's sinkings and asking for air support from the 15th onwards.

A Liberator appeared over the convoy in the late evening and, shortly afterwards, *Stork*, then ahead of the convoy, sighted a conning-tower ten miles on the convoy's starboard bow. The Liberator was sent off to attack and a few minutes later reported:

> Have attacked U-boat and scored seventeen hits. Enemy has either sunk or submerged.

Walker assumed the aircraft must have scored 'seventeen hits' with machine-gun fire. He could not imagine a U-boat diving if it had been hit that many times by anything larger. He tried to signal the aircraft for further information, but the Liberator had turned away and was heading out of sight.

There was every evidence that the 'pack' was still with them when darkness fell. At midnight, a lookout in *Stork* sighted a U-boat probing the defences astern. This was in *Stork*'s territory, so Walker proceeded to 'smarten him up nicely with my eight remaining depth-charges'. The attack was abortive and the sloop resumed her station. About the same time, *Gardenia*, with her stern damaged and her speed reduced to a maximum of ten knots, joined the screen.

The situation was not promising for the night. The escort was at its full strength of four ships but *Gardenia* was damaged;

she had no depth-charges; her asdic was useless and she had no speed to chase or attack; *Stork* had run out of depth-charges; *Marigold* would expend all her charges in the next attack; only *Convolvulus*, the patient shepherd during the absence of the others, was in a position to fight off enemy probes. Against this, the enemy could see four escorts and would not know their state of unreadiness.

Luckily, the next attack came from the starboard bow while *Convolvulus* was in a position ahead of the starboard column ship. She saw the U-boat racing in, trimmed down on the surface, and altered course at full speed to intercept. The startled U-boat about-turned promptly and with his superior speed was able to lose himself in the night.

After this episode the enemy threw in his hand and the rest of the night passed peaceably enough, marred only by a series of false alarms that left everyone weary and numb with strain when dawn broke on the 16th and brought the prospect of respite.

During the morning a Catalina flying boat arrived as their air escort for the day. At noon, Walker gave a striking demonstration of his contempt for the enemy by calling *Convolvulus* alongside him and, while both ships stopped, *Stork*'s motorboat was lowered and began transferring depth-charges from the corvette to replenish her empty racks. The wind had dropped and the seas had calmed down. The motor-boat made six trips carrying two depth-charges each time, before Walker decided the convoy had drawn far enough ahead and, to the audible relief of both crews, who expected to be torpedoed at any moment, had the boat hoisted inboard. Both ships had rejoined the convoy by the afternoon when a Whitley bomber came out to assist the Catalina.

With these reinforcements, Walker felt he could keep the U-boats submerged for the rest of the day, and he turned the convoy on a course that would take them the shortest way home. That night they waited expectantly for the enemy to attack, but nothing happened and for the first time in three days they began to hope for a rest.

But Doenitz had not yet finished with HG84. He had another weapon ready for just such an emergency.

Meanwhile, *Stork* had broken down with a painful disease known in naval circles as 'condenseritis' — a mechanical complaint which put one engine out of action until the trouble could be found and cured. She was reduced to a maximum speed of about nine knots, thereby joining *Gardenia* as a mere token escort. It was hardly surprising. For the last few days and nights the sloop had been flogged mercilessly, performing the duties of close escort and hunter until she had been driven, in Walker's own words, 'beyond the endurance of such a gallant thoroughbred'.

All day, the engine-room staff worked in an effort to find the fault while *Stork* and *Gardenia* could just keep pace with the convoy. This was the moment Doenitz chose to launch his next attack.

At 9.30 that evening, the destroyer *Wild Swan*, steaming some fifty miles to the eastwards, sighted nine enemy bombers flying towards the convoy. She signalled a general warning and, being in the path of their flight, engaged them with her anti-aircraft armament. The action was one of the fiercest air-sea battles involving a single surface unit ever fought in the war. The bombers attacked *Wild Swan* in waves of three. She was hit badly by the first wave, missed by the second and hit again by the third. But her vicious, determined fire broke up the formations and the aircraft returned singly. In the next ten minutes. *Wild Swan*, sinking by the stern, shot down six bombers before the remaining three broke off the action and flew out of sight. Only then did *Wild Swan* send out the news that she was sinking rapidly. One old destroyer,[10] veteran of the First World War, had broken up Doenitz's last attack on HG84.

The next two days, the convoy struggled northwards with fifty per cent of the escort limping in its wake, but, on the afternoon of the 19th, *Stork*'s engineer officer reported to the bridge that the patient had been cured. Walker increased speed on both engines and the little ship surged forward. They were just in time to greet an enemy aircraft which put in an appearance at the unprecedented time of 10.30 pm — an hour at which all good Focke-Wulfs should be asleep.

Delightedly, the guns' crews went into action to enjoy a practice shoot they had not been able for months to wheedle from the authorities. In what must have been a deadly reminder of his danger, the enemy pilot sheered away and scurried home with tiny puffs of black smoke threatening to burn his tail.

This was the last skirmish. The following day the convoy dispersed off the Clyde and Walker led his battered, tired little Group home to Liverpool.

Statistically, Convoy HG84 was not particularly successful. On the balance sheet were five valuable merchant ships and a Hurricane fighter lost for two probable 'kills' — for while Walker claimed *Gardenias* and his own attack the following night as two U-boats destroyed, they had not yet been confirmed.

---

[10] *Wild Swan*'s captain, Commander C. E. Slater, RN, survived the fury of this battle to receive the Distinguished Service Order.

When the Reports of Proceedings of the Group had been handed in at Liverpool, Walker fully expected to be called to account for his offensive tactics with such a small force. He was ready to acknowledge that the 'safe and timely arrival' of the convoy had at times hung by a thread, due to an entirely inadequate escort screen which on at least one occasion had consisted of only one ship, the corvette *Convolvulus*. He knew there were higher authorities who disapproved of his tactics and might use the debit balance sheet to relieve him of his command.

In his own Report, he had awarded credit and accepted blame for any mistakes someone, probably less experienced in the U-boat war, might consider he had made. Privately, he was proud of his Group and satisfied at their performance. If nothing else, the 36th Escort Group had proved itself a team thoroughly disciplined to his methods.

> I am proud [he said] of the offensive spirit, initiative, and sheer guts displayed by these corvettes. *Convolvulus*, my deputy during my absences from the convoy, never put a foot wrong. *Gardenia* displayed great tenacity despite her damage by remaining sixteen hours to witness the death of her U-boat. *Marigold* did some fine rescue work and lunged hard against shadowing U-boats when they came near to attacking *Copeland* who was carrying out her work of mercy. As for *Stork*, it is inspiring to command such a magnificent body of men, on their toes spoiling for a fight. I adopted an offensive policy in the belief that the best defence is to go out for kills.

He had nothing to fear. Neither the Commander-in-Chief nor the Director of Anti-Submarine Warfare assessed Battle Reports by the state of the balance sheet. They related Walker's actions to the weight of the enemy attack and the result was gratifying even to the most pessimistic. A deliberately planned massacre of Convoy HG84 had been averted. Instead of the almost total destruction hoped for by the enemy, the convoy had got through with only a twenty-two per cent loss.

Messages of congratulations were sent to *Stork*, but Walker shrugged them off. Far more important was the decisive fact that his unorthodox methods had stood up to vigorous analysis. He was impatient for the Group to carry out repairs. As soon as *Stork* could lead four of them to sea again, he would report ready for duty.

However, Sir Percy Noble had other plans for Commander Walker.

CHAPTER 7: MISSION TO 'CHOP'

The Navy in peacetime and the Navy at war are vastly different affairs. Officers who had been social lions and earmarked for high rank in 1939 had been known to fail on the battlefield; others who had spurned the niceties of the peacetime service and suffered for it were proving indomitable, and sometimes brilliant, leaders in war.

The Admiralty is probably the most rigidly disciplined of the three Service departments; yet time and again it proves itself capable of astonishingly human actions. Commanders-in-Chief are not responsible merely for the destruction of the enemy with the fleets at their disposal. They also keep a constant, vigilant watch over the health, behaviour, cares and worries of their commanding officers. Sir Percy Noble had long realized that in Commander Walker he had found one of the most keen and efficient U-boat hunters in the Western Approaches Command. He knew also, through that strange, invisible grapevine which reaches through mess decks and staffs, that Walker could best be rewarded by early promotion. Accordingly, he recommended to the Admiralty that the 36th Group's Senior Officer should be given immediately the rank of captain.

The Admiral had another motive for this. Reports had reached him through Staff channels that Walker, spending most of his sea time on *Stork*'s bridge from which he could instantly control any given emergency, was showing signs of strain and tiredness. He had summoned him to Derby House for an interview and had noticed for himself that the quiet, modest officer burned inside like a suppressed volcano when discussing the Atlantic battle. Tell-tale lines were already tugging at his eyes.

It was time for Walker to be rested ashore, but it was obvious too that any attempt to tell him so and relieve him for a trip would be strenuously resisted. If he were promoted he must expect to be moved from *Stork* and might accept a shore job, no matter how reluctantly, without realizing he was actually being given a let-up.

The Admiralty agreed with Sir Percy's recommendation and threw in a reward of its own. When the half-yearly promotion lists were issued in July, Walker's name headed the list of commanders promoted to captain, thereby cancelling out the pre-war report from *Valiant* which had criticized him. The citation read: *For leadership and skill in action against enemy submarines.*

Soon after this promotion, Sir Percy sent for his Chief of Staff, Commodore Mansfield, and said:

'Walker's promotion and seniority now makes it necessary to make some changes. Therefore I suggest we take the opportunity to rest him by appointing him Captain (D) for about six months. He should go back to sea by the spring of next year.'

Unaware of the real reason for his transfer ashore, this promotion brought disappointment to Walker. He saw the logic of the new appointment but was hardly content to sit behind a desk reading the exploits of the Western Approaches in their Battle Reports. When breaking the news to Eilleen, he said:

'The Admiralty have only themselves to blame if I make a damned awful Captain (D) — which I shall.'

He took over his new job in October and immediately opened a two-pronged attack on the Admiralty and the

Commander-in-Chief — one for a less cautious and more offensive approach to the Battle of the Atlantic, and the second to persuade Their Lordships that he should be sent back to sea in the small ships he had come to regard as his second home. He sent for Eilleen who gave up her job and they found 'The White House', South Road, Liverpool, which became their home for the remainder of the war — and his life.

His tall, spare figure with the gaunt, weather-tanned face became as familiar among the shopping crowds of the port as it was in the dockyards, inspecting ships, advising their commanders and sorting out the complex problems of getting old ships refitted, new ones launched and secret equipment installed in ships waiting to sail.

At Derby House, he analysed reports of convoy battles, handled personnel problems by the thousand, recommended officers and men for awards and sent for others to be quietly and politely burned by the 'bottles of acid' that became the standard reward for slovenly behaviour or indecision in action. Commanding officers learned that it was decisiveness that counted with Captain (D). He could not tolerate a dithering officer but would always help and advise those whose decisions had been near to disastrous.

On a few occasions, he was invited to wardroom celebration parties and it was then that his gayer, more relaxed, side appeared in the intimacy of a close professional circle. He had always been keen on physical exercise and keeping fit generally — he took cold baths winter and summer — and he could stand on his head almost indefinitely, drinking a glass of beer.

At Christmas, Walker gave the first of his few wartime lectures. It was on a subject he believed in passionately and which he considered a number of reservist commanding officers should know more about.

'Leadership comes very much easier to those of strong personality, commanding presence, but don't fall into the mistake of thinking these things are essential. They are not. Nelson and Napoleon were both little squirts and Hitler is in my opinion a figure of fun. Yet Napoleon led a whole nation for some years all over Europe to eventual defeat and Hitler is doing the same thing now.

'There is a distinction between leadership and discipline. An utterly undisciplined rabble was successfully led to storm the Bastille in 1789 — leadership without discipline. Conversely, I have watched a magnificently disciplined body of Royal Marines in a big ship expending foot-tons of energy in trivial exercises — discipline without leadership. A well-led ship's company can be recognized in any emergency by their ready and intelligent *anticipation of orders and the absence of confusion and shouting.*'

Unconsciously, perhaps, he was drawing upon his own experience in command. It was against the wasting of 'foot-tons of energy' that he had rebelled in big ships before the war. Similarly, he could not really care how a sailor dressed at sea or whether his hair was cut to the required length, so long as he was keen, efficient and trustworthy in his job.

On morale, he dealt mainly from his own experiences quoting examples from *Stork* and current cases he was dealing with at Derby House.

'I have seen a good many leave-breakers, ship-jumpers, drunks, etc,' he said. 'I have a standard speech for them. I tell them what stinking skunks they are for helping the German war effort, doing their little best to lose the Battle of the Atlantic, miserably failing their country in her hour of need.

Most of them are shaken to the core by it, some even burst into tears.

'You must get home to your men that there is no excuse for leave-breaking, that it is not merely playing truant from school but letting their mates down badly. If a wife is ill or having a baby, the man must realize that his duty to his country comes before his duty to his family.

'Another cause of low morale is the difference in pay between the sailor and the dockyard and factory workers ashore. Rub in the honour of being picked for the finest fighting team in the world — and that the country would have been in German hands long ago but for that team and his part in it.'

Some weeks before, Timothy had written asking his father to help him transfer to submarines. Walker had pulled a few minor strings and at Christmas his son, now a sub-lieutenant RNVR, came home to Liverpool on leave prior to attending a submarine course at Blyth. Nicholas was also on leave, and Gillian had taken a job at a garage to learn something about driving before joining the Wrens. As Timmy had been in Rome when Andrew was born, this meant that the family was together for the first time.

One night during the festivities, Eilleen wakened and heard a slight noise outside her bedroom. She slipped out of bed, opened the door and to her astonishment saw a workman's brazier glowing redly on the landing and, in front of it, a large red-painted signpost saying road closed. She returned to the bedroom, shook Johnnie awake and told him what she had seen. 'Nicholas,' he muttered sleepily. 'I'll deal with him in the morning.' Then he turned over and went to sleep again, leaving Eilleen prey to such thoughts as a mother might have at 2 am with a brazier burning enthusiastically on her landing.

At breakfast next morning, Nicholas and Gillian glanced apprehensively at their father who continued to sip his coffee in silence. He finished a second cup and lit a cigarette before looking at Nicholas and saying abruptly:

'Put it back.'

He walked out leaving consternation behind him. It had not seemed such a bad idea to remove the brazier after a party at night; but to put it back in cold blood during daylight was another matter. Yet family discipline was such that after dusk that evening, two heavily-laden figures slunk furtively through the streets towards the river. A splash in the Mersey covered their trail and the incident was closed.

Walker's reputation as a fighting captain and a relentless administrator was so well known that when Admiral Sir Max Horton took over the Western Approaches from Sir Percy Noble, who was being sent to Washington for liaison duties, one of the first officers he asked to see was Captain (D). It was to be one of many meetings and, by the time Walker returned to sea, Sir Max Horton had set his standard of efficiency for the Command on the level of this captain.

More important to Walker, he found the new Commander-in-Chief sympathetic to his ideas for more positive action in the Atlantic Battle. He set seriously to work on a paper campaign directed at both the Admiral and the Admiralty to convince them that the U-boat war could not be won by escorts huddled round convoys and waiting for the enemy.

In a series of memoranda, he stressed the need for special groups to roam the Atlantic freely in search of the enemy. Coastal Command, he said, were increasing the number of their aircraft and, as a result, air cooperation was being improved and extended right across the Bay of Biscay, up to Iceland and over to Greenland.

Now was the time for sloops and destroyers to revert to their traditional roles of seeking out and destroying the enemy. He pointed to dockyards round the country where new ships were nearing completion and urged that these should be used to form the new striking forces, or hunting groups.

During one discussion with Sir Max Horton, the latter asked: 'And where would you suggest these hunting groups would find the enemy?'

'In my view we should seek them out on their own doorstep, the Bay of Biscay, and the mid-Atlantic where they are also vulnerable because they feel safe.'

'That's around the "Chop" Line Area,'[11] said Sir Max. 'Without aircraft you might spend days not sighting a damn thing. You would need to take a carrier, and I doubt if we could afford to risk them in that kind of operation.'

Curiously, although he agreed with Walker on almost every point in the general plan, the Commander-in-Chief refused to add his endorsement on the question of aircraft-carriers. But, at the Admiralty, this was no problem. Small carriers were being built in considerable numbers and the war at sea was becoming the pivot of all other military operations.

Sir Max went to London for a series of conferences and, by February, Walker's ideas were substantially approved. They were not his alone. Other senior officers had contributed the basis of much of the overall plan and little could have been done without the help of Sir Max Horton. But it was Walker's persistence and energy that pushed it through.

He received forceful backing from Naval Intelligence, who compiled reports from numerous sources into composite

[11] The Atlantic was divided down the middle by the 'Chop' Line. To the west of 'Chop' the Americans had control, east of 'Chop' was Britain's responsibility.

monthly surveys of the Battle of the Atlantic for the private use of the War Cabinet, Board of the Admiralty and certain departmental heads, such as the Director of Anti-Submarine Warfare and the Commander-in-Chief of the various shore and seagoing commands.

The Survey for January 1943 was hardly encouraging.

> Now that Grand Admiral Doenitz is Supreme Commander of the German Navy [said the Intelligence Report] we may expect all units to operate in support of the U-boat war and we shall be on the lookout for any indication of a change of policy. It is certainly going to be a grim fight in 1943 and though we are not as ready as we would like to be, there have been plenty of examples late in 1942 to demonstrate that even with our present inadequate air and surface escorts, with good training and team work it is possible to fight a convoy through a pack of U-boats and give as good as we get.[12]

For March and February the Reports were equally, if not slightly more, cheerless.

> Never before has the enemy displayed such single-mindedness of purpose in utilizing his strength against one objective — the interruption of supplies from America to Great Britain. As a result, engagements were embittered and successes against U-boats high.
>
> The months ahead are critical and the outcome of the struggle is by no means sure.

It was at this vital period that Walker persuaded Sir Max Horton to let him return to the struggle.

He was appointed captain of a new sloop, *Starling*, and senior officer of the now famous Atlantic striking force known as the

---

[12] Intelligence was referring to Walker's defence of convoy HG76

Second Support Group, consisting of five other sloops of the same class — *Wild Goose, Wren, Kite, Cygnet* and *Woodpecker*.

There was no conflict in his mind over leaving his family again. He knew his wife would never attempt to hold him back even if she could. For Eilleen, his return to sea meant going back to the long days and weeks of waiting she had come to share with thousands of naval wives throughout the country, never quite certain what the next telegram or BBC announcement would bring. She still suffered from a recurrent illness, but if she were troubled in any way, Johnnie was not allowed to see it.

Her patient restraint when her husband was ashore did not escape him. He knew she was calling on all resources of mind and body to appear cheerful at times when she must have felt more like crying. Before leaving the office of Captain (D), Walker proposed to broadcast a message to all Navy wives. This was accepted by the BBC and then quashed by the Admiralty who feared it might tend to convey to the world that we had so many deserters and leave-breakers that we had to appeal to their women to help. In fact, Walker wanted the help of the Navy wives and sweethearts, not because of deserting — they were too few cases to worry about — but because he wished these women to realize how important they were in maintaining the morale of the fighting men. He considered they were as vital to the war effort as anyone in the factories.

Today, many of those women who were sweethearts are wives now, and a great number of the wives have become mothers. For some nostalgic memories may return at this brief excerpt from Captain Walker's message.

> We sailors all know that beastly moment when leave is over
> and how it would be tempting to seize on some trivial excuse
> to stay a little longer. I am glad to say that most wives see to it

that their husbands return to their ships in good time. I have this to say to those who have wavered. Never forget your influence on your man and keep him up to the mark. Send him back from leave itching to get at Hitler's throat — not unhappy, worried and anxious about his home. Your paramount duty is to help your husband or son or sweetheart to grind the Nazi face back into the dirt from which it sprang.

Soon after handing over office to his relief, Walker put in a request that with only a few exceptions the whole crew, officers and men, of *Stork* should be appointed to *Starling*, Most of them had been paid off from *Stork* when she passed into dockyard hands, and were now on leave. Telegrams went out from Derby House ordering as many as were available to report to Fairfield's Dockyard near Glasgow to standby Job Number SL197.

Fairfield's was soon working overtime. Job Number SL197, an embryo ship which by the end of March, 1943, was to become the sloop-of-war, HMS *Starling*, was not only needed urgently by the Admiralty, but even more so by Captain John Walker, whose letter to the management left them in no doubt at all of the fate awaiting them if the ship were delayed in any way.

For the next two weeks, SL197 was the focal point for hundreds of workers. Rivetters clattered and chattered their deafening way along the hull; welders' lamps hissed defiance at the daily drizzle; railway goods wagons clanged alongside, shunted there by noisily officious engines; towering cranes trundled crazily up and down in whining unison, their giraffe-like arms swaying drunkenly skywards.

The bare-ribbed carcass of rusting metal became a red paint-splotched shell stuffed daily with engines and instruments of war, while bits of superstructure appeared round a stumpy, grotesque mast. Keeping wondering eyes on this magical transformation of jumbled confusion of scrap metal into the recognizable shape of a ship were Lieutenant Impey, former asdic officer of *Stork*, Lieutenant John Filleul, RN, and Sub-Lieutenant Alan Burn, RNVR, a newcomer to the Walker entourage. As 'standby' officers waiting for the time to walk aboard, they lived in a hotel ashore by night and in a tiny wooden hut in the Yard by day. They did not quite know what would emerge from the muddy inferno Job Number SL197.

Filleul, newly promoted, was overjoyed at his appointment to the embryo *Starling*, Ever since he had sailed in *Stork* and returned from the fierce, drawn-out defence of convoy HG84, he had become a fervent supporter of his captain. While on leave, he had received the telegram appointing him to *Starling*, Next he learned that most of *Stork*'s crew were also being transferred at the request of their new commanding officer.

During the long evenings ashore waiting for SL197 to become a ship with a name, Filleul told stories of *Stork* and Walker to Alan Burn, a stocky, square-faced recent arrival to Western Approaches Command who had heard of his new commanding officer and imagined him a stickler for discipline and not at all likely to tolerate mistakes a reservist officer might be expected to make — particularly from such a key department head as the Gunnery Officer.

At last came March 21st, Commissioning Day, and those key officers and ratings who had watched a ship grow from the tangled chaos of Fairfield's gazed in wonderment again at the sleek, newly-painted warship with bristling guns and businesslike equipment giving her the appearance of a healthy warrior impatiently waiting for the order that would fling him into the line.

To Walker, this day meant a long-delayed return to the Atlantic battlefield. He knew some of the faces confronting him on the quarterdeck as he addressed the ship's company. On brief acquaintance with those officers he had met for the first time, he was satisfied there would be no hitches to prevent the working-up trials being cut shorter than usual. He was particularly pleased that Lieutenant Impey, RN, his asdic officer in *Stork*, had been sent to *Starling* as First Lieutenant.

His Commission Speech was short — most of these men knew what he wanted of them — and after the officers had exchanged handshakes with the Yard superintendents the bo'sun's mate piped:

'Secure for sea. All hands prepare for leaving harbour. Sea-duty men to their stations.'

A few minutes later, the engines throbbed alive and HMS *Starling*, at last a ship with a name instead of a number, sailed down the Clyde on her maiden voyage to the Western Approaches. Hundreds of workers lined the docksides to wave and shout 'good luck', for they were as proud of the ship as the crew who now sailed in her.

While steaming down the Clyde they received a general signal from Commander-in-Chief, Western Approaches, to all units in the Command saying it was intended to operate five support Groups over the North Atlantic convoy routes, and Initial Groups would proceed to sea on March 24th. These would remain under operational control of C-in-C Western Approaches regardless of 'Chop'.

The officers of *Starling* now received some idea of what their duties were to be. Walker already knew, but his eye was fixed on the Bay. He would go along with the plan to support the convoy escorts for the moment, but his main target for the future operations was Biscay itself.

For the next ten days it was trials, exercises, exercises and trials for the crew of *Starling*. From the first Captain Walker made it clear to officers and men that their job in the war was to sink U-boats, and everything was directed to achieve the highest possible competence in this art; day and night this single, simple idea of 'kill the Boche before he kills you' drove *Starling*'s crew to semi-exhaustion until one day they sailed from Liverpool, a confident, keen fighting unit ready for war, impatient to get into the battlefield to seek out and destroy the enemy.

At the end of April, they received their orders. The other five ships of the Second Support Group — *Wild Goose*, *Wren*, *Kite*, *Cygnet* and *Woodpecker* — had completed their training and were to meet their leader off Londonderry whence they were to proceed to the mid-Atlantic. The strategic plan to harry the U-boat on their doorstep and in their happiest hunting ground along the mid-Atlantic 'Chop' Line was about to be launched.

The Second Support Group became a striking force on April 28th when the six sloops left the Western Approaches bound for the Atlantic deepfield where, free from troublesome aircraft, the U-boats lay in wait for the convoys. Added to Walker's satisfaction at being on his own bridge again, was the pleasure of knowing that in command of *Wild Goose* was his old friend, Commander D. E. G. Wemyss.

In his first tour of the Battle of the Atlantic, Walker had been a convoy escort drawing the enemy like a magnet. Now he was looking for trouble wherever it could be found. After two days' steaming he was ordered to take his Group to assist a convoy inward bound from Halifax, Nova Scotia, which was being hard-pressed by a U-boat 'wolf pack'.

The Group made contact the following evening and spread themselves in a wide circle round both convoy and its close escort, acting as scouts to keep shadowing U-boats down where their slow speed would soon give the convoy a chance to draw ahead out of the trap. For the next three nights there were a series of alarms which gave the six sloops little more satisfaction than the chance to work together for the first time as a unit. Walker kept them in hunting formation exercises, both by day and night, giving the commanding officers the opportunity to learn his methods of handling six ships as one.

In each ship, individual drills ironed out the dockyard faults and accustomed the crew to new equipment. In *Starling*, small defects became apparent with monotonous regularity and both officers and men expended a more than usual amount of blood, sweat and bad language before Walker announced with some irony that he might yet turn them into a crew fit to go to war. Alan Burn felt there was some justification for his captain's attitude when, during a practice shoot, he gave the order 'Open Fire', and instead of the deafening crack of the four-inch twin guns exploding into flame, there was a painful and deathly silence.

The textbook said that, before taking any further action, he should order 'Cease Fire'. So, controlling his mounting anger at this strange inefficiency from his department, he shouted down the telephone to all guns:

'Cease Firing.'

Immediately, the guns roared into action sending a salvo of shells hurtling over the grey Atlantic. From his action station on the bridge, Burn turned hesitantly and with some embarrassment to see how Walker had received this tendency of his gunnery people instantly to reverse orders, and was astonished to find his captain and the first lieutenant chuckling.

On the fourth night, the Group left the convoy to take up its patrol where Walker exercised them again and again in zigzag and hunting manoeuvres and in drills designed to meet any emergency. Officers of the Watch found life anything but peaceful with a captain who might suddenly interrupt a peaceful afternoon by throwing a lifebuoy overboard and shouting: 'That's a man overboard. Pick him up without lowering the boat.' When this tricky piece of ship handling had been accomplished, Walker would order: 'Tell all ships to fire a depth-charge set to a hundred feet.'

He would time each ship and send rudely informative signals to those he considered had taken too long to get their charges away. At night, he would liven up proceedings by suddenly telling the Officers of the Watch: 'U-boat on the starboard bow. Illuminate it with starshell.' If there were any delay, the officer was left in no doubt of what Walker thought of him. This was a favourite test and took place in nearly every watch, for Walker hoped that U-boats would see the starshell and come rushing towards him to find out what was happening.

He varied it by leaving the bridge and, while passing through the wheelhouse below, ordered the helmsman to put the wheel hard over one way or the other and report to the Officer of the Watch that it had jammed. He waited and timed the hapless officer's reactions. Gradually, the officers grew to anticipate these 'stunt' alarms and a friendly rivalry sprang up in the wardroom to see who could react the quickest. This mood passed down to the men, and the gun crews or depth-charge crew of each watch would gloat wickedly over an unfortunate team which had carried out a drill only a fraction of a second slower.

In this way, the dirt of the dockyard fell away from *Starling* and, at the end of this first uneventful voyage, the guns could fire salvoes of six rounds in thirty seconds and the depth-charge crews could fire a pattern of ten charges in fifteen seconds.

The First Lieutenant maintained acidly that these were rotten performances, although Walker grinned his satisfaction. Confidence ran through the mess decks like a smooth, vintage wine and bubbled over into keen inter-ship rivalry uniting the Group in a burning determination to come to grips with the enemy.

Early in the morning of May 12th, the Group were steaming off Northern Ireland on their way to Liverpool. The most excited officer in *Starling* was John Filleul. If there were time before they sailed again he intended to marry a girl who, having said 'Yes', now waited in Bournemouth for him to say when the Navy could spare him for those few days necessary to organize the ceremony and a brief honeymoon.

Then Walker took a hand. It was a strict rule that no ship at sea should break wireless silence except in clearly defined circumstances — one of which gave commanding officers a measure of discretion, and leaders of Groups even a little more. As captain of *Starling* and Leader of the Second Support Group, he used this discretion. He sent a wireless signal addressed to Captain (D), Liverpool, requesting that Miss Wendy Taylor in Bournemouth be informed that her fiancé was due in harbour that evening. She should proceed immediately with arrangements for the earliest possible wedding.

By the time Filleul telephoned her in the evening, she had the situation under control. The wedding went off without a hitch next morning followed by a three days' honeymoon. In Liverpool, Captain Walker found his Commander-in-Chief, who had received a copy of the signal, unwilling to condone his use of personal discretion in breaking wireless silence for a private and domestic reason. If he was temporarily in hot water, Walker did not mind. It was more important that his officers and men should be happy at home — in his view the root of fighting efficiency at sea.

Four days later they sailed again to act as a striking force along the northern convoy routes, clearing the shipping lanes of patrolling U-boats in wait to intercept our east-and westbound convoys.

June 1st dawned clear and sunny. The grey Atlantic had for once stopped heaving and lay placid and oily under a hot sun shining brilliantly from a blue, cloudless sky. The 900 men of the Second Support Group threw aside their salt-caked duffle coats, damp sweaters and woollen socks for clean white singlets and uniform trousers.

In *Starling* there was little to disturb the peaceful calm of such an unexpectedly glorious day. The sea rushed quietly past the bows in frivolous curling waves; an occasional clanking of buckets came from the decks where sailors were washing down paintwork; from the gun platform in front of and below the bridge came the steady hum of conversation as the crews on watch stripped and examined the mechanism. The elements had called a truce, Neptune was on holiday and *Starling* could relax. To Alan Burn, the Officer of the Watch, it seemed more like a summer's day on a vicarage lawn.

'You know, John,' said he blissfully, 'I can almost hear the sound of tennis rackets hitting the ball over the net and see myself having tea on the lawn accompanied by the drone of wasps and bees. Marvellous thought.'

Suddenly, a telephone buzzer blared urgently. Burn sprang to the receiver.

'What is it?'

'Submarine on the surface transmitting on bearing 225 degrees. Must be about twenty miles away, Sir.'

It was the HF/DF operator reporting that his set was intercepting a U-boat chattering either to its base or another colleague. Burn snapped out his order.

'Port fifteen ... midships ... steady ... steer 225. Full speed ahead both.'

He turned to the voice pipe reaching down to the captain's sea cabin.

'Captain, Sir.'

'Yes, what is it?' came the muffled reply.

'Submarine on the surface reported by HF/DF.'

'Right.'

In a few seconds, Walker was on the bridge, checking the orders given by Alan and sending signals to the Group. The six ships were reformed in line abreast on their new course along the bearing of the U-boat, steaming at full speed.

The tempo in *Starling* changed swiftly. She vibrated violently as the engines raced and thousands of fittings began to throb in protest. Walker turned to Burn. 'Sound Action Stations.' To the Yeoman of Signals: 'Make to the Group: *keep station on me. Course 225, speed 18 knots, ships to be four miles apart.*'

As he spoke, the alarm bells clanged through the ship and in seconds the decks were filled with seamen in every state of dress — or undress — dashing to their action stations.

A lamp blinked from *Wild Goose* and the Yeoman read out:
Have picked up U-boat on HF/DF bearing 228.

Just then *Starling*'s HF/DF officer reported the U-boat still talking on a bearing 225. The navigator quickly ran off the two nearly parallel lines on his chart and placed the enemy between fifteen and twenty miles away.

It was their first smell of the enemy since leaving the builders' yard.

Walker noted in his Diary:

> I fixed the U-boat's position using bearings from *Starling* and *Wild Goose*. The date was June 1st, the Christian name of my HF/DF officer was Howe, asdic conditions were perfect — all these things promised well.

At 10.15, lookouts in *Starling* sighted a swirl of water and, almost at once, her asdic team picked up an echo that was unmistakably a submarine.

CHAPTER 8: BLOCKADE

Twelve months earlier, on May 27th, 1942, a lithe, fair-haired young officer had been ushered into the private office of Admiral Doenitz at U-boat headquarters in Lorient. He was Kapitanleutnant Hans Linder, commanding officer of the new 500-ton submarine, *U-202*, and he had been summoned to a briefing for a secret mission.

'This job is going to take a lot of nerve and cool judgement, Linder,' Doenitz said. 'Your navigation will have to be exact. One mistake might cost the lives of you all and, whatever the cost, you must not lose your boat or your crew. Is that clear?'

Linder nodded.

'Right. You are to take four secret agents with their equipment to the American coast and land them on Long Island, New Jersey. The actual spot is the beach at Amagansett. You should put them ashore on June 13th and in any event not later than the 15th. Those dates coincide with the new moon which you will need for an approach so close inshore, although you must risk being sighted by some wide-awake coastguard. Remember, the safety of your boat and your crew comes before the lives of the four spies.'

'I understand, Sir,' replied Linder excitedly. 'When do I sail?'

'The passengers join you today. You sail tomorrow.'

'Yes, Sir.' Linder saluted and returned to his boat to prepare for the voyage.

When Linder took *U-202* to sea next day, he did not know he was in the van of a determined German effort to invade the United States with fifteen highly-trained saboteurs and intelligence agents whose mission was to organize a nationwide espionage network. The same afternoon, *U-584* sailed with five more spies bound for Jacksonville while another U-boat was embarking six others to be landed near Boston. The last group never sailed, but nine agents were already on their way across the Atlantic.

This special mission, planned by German Military Intelligence and given the code name 'Operation Pastorius', was designed to establish secret wireless communication between Germany and America; to provide the nucleus of a spy organization responsible for supplying general intelligence; to set up a secret saboteur school which would supervise the blowing up of vital military establishments; and to infiltrate into those circles best calculated to be of use in undermining the morale of the people.

The agents were volunteers chosen because they had intimate knowledge of the United States, having lived there or visited the country before the war. One claimed to have lived in New York throughout the First World War, operating as a German spy. But while waiting for the U-boat arm to cany them across the Atlantic, several had consumed too much French wine at Lorient and loosened tongues revealed their real purpose in volunteering. At least three said they intended to give themselves up to the United States Police and spend the remainder of the war in the comparative luxury of a POW camp, apparently preferring this to the Russian front.

Reports of their behaviour reached Doenitz who was angered at the thought of risking valuable U-boats for the sake of transporting such characters. In a signal to Berlin, he said: 'There is every evidence that the special agents are not activated by patriotic motives but rather by adventurous spirits and a desire to seek refuge in the United States. I request "Operation Pastorius" be considered in this light because we cannot on any account risk unduly and with little chance of reward the loss of the submarine involved in their transportation.'[13]

Military intelligence, however, had spent many months and plenty of money in training the saboteur force and was not to be swayed by a 'lay' report from Lorient. Doenitz was ordered to proceed with the operation as planned. Having given instructions to *U-202* and *U-584*, he managed to effect a compromise by seizing on slight engine trouble in the third U-boat to postpone her sailing for so long that the six agents had their orders cancelled.

On board *U-202*, her four passengers changed into civilian clothes labelled with the name of a well-known New York department store. They carried forged papers and passports, and each was equipped with a brief case into which was stowed explosives in the shape of highly-inflammable 'stick' grenades and various parts of two wireless transmitting and receiving sets. Between them they carried 500 dollars, a list of 'sympathetic addresses' and the names of hotels suitable for visitors who wanted to remain as inconspicuous as possible.

Linder made the crossing on the surface, when out of range of air patrols, and submerged on approaching the United States coast. On the evening of June 13th he lay at periscope depth off the entrance to Long Island Sound in New York harbour. It was a brilliant summer's day and the sun went down reluctantly. The four spies took it in turns to look through the periscope at passing ships and chuckled among themselves as they joked with the U-boat's crew about what they would do on their first night ashore as self-appointed members of the American community.

---

[13] Admiralty Intelligence.

According to one member of the crew: 'Our passengers seemed to have been told in Berlin that every American girl looked like a Hollywood film star and would be easier to pick up than a French harlot.'

Darkness fell shortly before 11 pm and Linder surfaced for the approach towards the coast. Apart from the new moon, navigation was made easy by the bright lights ashore reflecting on the water and at midnight they were close enough to hear the blaring of car horns and the strains of dance music. Silently, a rubber dinghy was lowered into the water from the foredeck and the four spies, waving good-bye to the officers on the conning-tower, took their places while three of Linder's sailors rowed them ashore.

They landed on Amagansett beach at exactly thirty minutes after midnight, picked up their brief cases, and, after shaking hands with the sailors, vanished across the beach into the dark hinterland of the American continent. At almost the same moment, five of their colleagues were landed on a beach near Jacksonville, from *U-584*.[14]

When his rubber dinghy had been safely hauled inboard, Linder let out a deep breath of relief and muttered aloud: 'Thank heaven that's over.' He turned *U-202* seawards for the safety of open sea; but two minutes later the U-boat shuddered and the crew were shocked into near-panic by a horrible grating noise which seemed to echo through the night. *U-202* was stuck hard and fast on a sandbank on an ebb tide.

Despite continued frantic efforts to refloat her during the night, she remained firmly embedded. Linder sent a signal to Lorient informing Doenitz that he had successfully carried out

---

[14] Both groups ran into coastal patrols and were arrested. All nine were charged with espionage and six were sent to the electric chair. The remaining three received life imprisonment.

his mission but could not return and had prepared to surrender his men to imprisonment. Then he instructed the crew to set scuttling charges, and settled down to await daylight.

At the first greyness of dawn they heard again the loud blaring of car horns; dogs barked and cocks crowed. Luckily, although on the surface, they were hidden by a heavy mist which lay over the sea, blotting out the coastline. Gradually the tide turned and began to flow strongly. At 5 am the boat shifted slightly. Linder ordered the crew to sea stations and put both engines astern at full power. Slowly the U-boat moved over the sand, quivering as the propellers gripped the water and strained to pull her clear. Suddenly, the bows shot up and she surged backwards, clear at last. Still cloaked by the mist, Linder headed seawards and made good his escape.[15]

This mission cracked Linder's nerve and, on return to Brest, he was relieved by Kapitanleutnant Gunter Poser, who became commanding officer of one of Doenitz's most favoured U-boats.

Under Poser, *U-202* made five more voyages, sinking a total of 50,000 tons of Allied shipping before sailing from Brest on April 29th, 1943, on her ninth trip of the war. She was to patrol in the vicinity of the northern convoy routes in mid-Atlantic.

During May she was bombed by aircraft, chased by escorts and made several abortive attacks on convoys. Poser, aged twenty-seven, and fairly quick-witted, was a capable captain but a lazy one. He failed to press home his attacks, preferred to lie in wait for targets rather than look for them, and spent most of his time at sea lying on his bunk reading and dozing. On May

---

[15] The incident was told to Naval Intelligence Officers, who interrogated the survivors of *U-202*, and was confirmed by captured documents.

27th, he was ordered to return to Brest to take fuel on board before sailing to Kiel for a refit. Thankfully, he headed *U-202* for the Bay of Biscay and began planning his leave.

In her thirty days at sea, *U-202* had been bombed three times, had dived for twenty-nine aircraft alarms and had been chased five times by escorts.

At 10 am on June 1st, a chief petty officer acting as Officer of the Watch sighted mastheads which he took to belong to a convoy. He reported to Poser, who was lying on his bunk, and was told to take *U-202* closer to the convoy. Eventually, Poser decided to look for himself. On the conning-tower he glanced through his binoculars and went suddenly rigid.

'My God,' he shouted. 'I can't see any merchant ships, only destroyers. Sound diving stations.'

Klaxons clattered through the U-boat and within seconds she was diving to 500 feet. Poser ordered all machinery except the electric lighting generators and engines to be shut down and waited hopefully for the destroyers to pass overhead. He could not be expected to know that he had not seen destroyers, but the sloops of the Second Support Group, already sweeping with their asdics. And in *Starling*, the asdic officer, Lieutenant Impey, had already reported: 'In contact, Sir.'

As he rapped out orders to be signalled to the Group, Walker seemed to come alive with an energy and drive quite new to the old hands from the *Stork* days. They remembered the grin on his face at the first signs of battle; they remembered the light of sheer joy in his eyes at the prospect of a 'kill'; now there was a tenseness about him as though he were trying to steer the asdic on to the target by will power alone. He stood behind the compass, completely at home in this struggle, his mind racing ahead to anticipate the evasive tactics his opponent might use. Concern about a possible enemy counterattack never entered Walker's head.

'Yeoman, tell *Cygnet*, *Woodpecker* and *Wren* to maintain square patrol at two miles and *Wild Goose* and *Kite* to stand by in the outfield to support my attack.'

He turned to the asdic officer.

'Going in to attack now.'

His orders to the wheelhouse for full speed were made quietly.

Starling surged forward, pulsating with power, and her bows cutting foaming waves through the placid sea, her wide white-edged wake vanishing almost imperceptibly into the glassy, even breathing of the swell astern. The 'ping' of the asdic beam echoing from the hull of *U-202* came faster as the range shortened.

'Stand by depth-charges...': a second later.... 'FIRE'.

Tons of high explosives rolled from the stern rails and were shot from throwers on either side of the quarter deck to curve gracefully into the air. In all, ten charges were rumbling downwards through the water heading for the hidden enemy. For a few seconds there was silence. Then miles of ocean and the waiting sloops shook and quivered under the blasting as the charges went off in a series of deafening, crackling roars. Huge columns of water boiled to the surface and sprayed out into vast fountains astern of *Starling*. The great cascades of water subsided, leaving spreading whirlpools to mark the position of the attack. But there was no U-boat.

Walker settled down to the struggle. His adversary was proving tough to hold and hard to find; he admired an enemy who refused to be panicked into some desperate folly that would lead to easy and swift destruction.

He took *Starling* out for half a mile and turned to regain contact. Next, he ordered *Wild Goose* and *Kite* to join him while the other three sloops kept up their patrol ready to pick up the U-boat should she shake off her attackers.

Five hundred feet below, the crew of *U-202* picked themselves up from the corners into which they had been flung by the force of the depth-charges. Everything movable had been smashed; the lights had failed, and a small leak had appeared in the stern. They had been saved by the inaccuracies of the depth-charge mechanism, which had been set to 350 and 550 feet but had probably exploded fifty feet either way. Poser began to wonder if this was an attack he could escape and, for the first time, the crew thought it likely that they would have been better off had they surrendered off the beach at Amagansett a year before. Poser turned to his engineer and ordered:

'Take her up to 400.'

During *Starling*'s working-up trials, Walker had devised a depth-charge barrage attack for use against U-boats believed to be hugging extreme depths for safety. The plan, known as 'Operation Plaster', called for three ships in close line abreast to drop depth-charges set to 550 feet at five-second intervals.

Now he signalled *Wild Goose* and *Kite* to close in on either side of *Starling* and the three ships steamed forwards over the 'pinged' position of the U-boat dropping a continuous stream of depth-charges. It was the naval equivalent of the artillery barrage that precedes an infantry attack. The sea heaved and boiled under the non-stop impact of the explosions. Twisting and turning and always leaving a trail of charges, the ships 'plastered' the area of *U-202*. In three minutes a total of seventy-six depth-charges had rocked and shaken the attacking ships almost as much as it had the U-boat.

Poser, hearing the first of the barrage explode beneath him, at first thought his hunters outwitted. After minutes of continuous shuddering blasts threatening to blow out every rivet, he decided to dive as deep as *U-202* could go. He gave his orders calmly, while the sweat streamed down his face.

'Slow ahead both engines ...

'Diving ...

'Take her down slowly....'

Tautly the control room crew watched the depth gauge. How far down would she go; and could they get below the rolling roar of depth-charges? The engineer officer called out the reading:

'Five hundred ... 550 ... 600 ... 650 ... 700.' That was the limit she had taken on exercises. Much more, and she would crack under the tremendous pressure.

'Seven hundred and fifty feet ...'

The first lieutenant muttered hoarsely into the silence.

'For heaven's sake, Sir, she won't take any more. Let's stay here or surface and fight it out. She'll break up at any moment if we go farther.'

Poser ignored the plea and went on staring rigidly at the controls, his mind concentrating on the creaks and groans reverberating through the boat from the straining hull.

'Seven hundred and eighty ... 800 ....' Now it was the engineer's turn to plead with his captain.

'With the weight of water on top now, Sir, she probably won't go up. For the love of God, no farther.'

Still there was silence from Poser. Above they could hear the dull explosions of the depth-charges cushioned by a gap of 300 feet of ocean. It was not the depth-charges that would worry them now: only that the U-boat would hold together.

'Eight hundred and twenty feet, Sir.'

Poser snapped out a command.

'Level off and keep her trimmed at 820. Steer due north with revolutions for three knots.'

He left the control room abruptly and the amazed crew saw him take off his jacket, collapse on his bunk and begin reading. He called out to the first lieutenant.

'Warn the crew to use as little energy as possible and to talk only when necessary. The more we conserve our air the longer we can stay down. The enemy might leave us alone or lose us in a few hours.'

There was little hope of that. Above, Walker took *Starling* in for a second attack with charges set at 300 feet. When this had little effect, he called in *Wild Goose* and *Kite* again and the three ships set off on a second barrage attack. The only damage inflicted was to blow *Kite*'s gyro compass out of action, and Walker sent her into the outfield, bringing in *Woodpecker* to take her place.

Woodpecker carried out a single attack also without result and Walker turned to the officers on *Starling*'s bridge. 'Now we have established that he isn't too shallow, we can only assume he must be deeper than we thought.'

He made several test runs on asdic bearing and found he was losing the echo each time at a range of 700 yards. This meant the U-boat was deeper than 500 feet. 'What I wouldn't give,' he exclaimed to all and sundry, 'for a good and large charge capable of being set to 700 feet.' He had no idea at that time — neither had the Admiralty — that U-boats could withstand the pressure of water at more than 800 feet.

As the day wore on, Walker maintained asdic contact in *Starling* and, using the loudhailer, directed his Group into a series of attacks at speeds of little more than five knots. Between attacks he did everything possible to 'rattle the U-boat into using up his batteries'. He carried out dummy attacks at speed hoping the enemy would hear his fast-revving propellers and use up valuable battery power in taking avoiding action. Then he ordered *Kite* to drop charges in the outfield to give the impression the Group was drawing away on a false scent.

Kapitanleutnant Poser was also using every trick he knew. U-boats had been equipped with a device that could be fired from torpedo tubes which caused a minor upheaval in the water and sent huge bubbles upwards and gave off the same echo on an asdic set as the U-boat itself. In this way it was hoped that the asdic 'ping' would receive an echo back from the device, which would be attacked and the ships further led astray by the appearance of bubbles. They were known as Submarine Bubble Targets — SBTs. Poser ordered them to be released every few minutes throughout the day to hide his alterations of course.

Walker had a knack of knowing when his asdic operators were 'pinging' off a U-boat or an SBT. Between 10.30 am and 7 pm *U-202* released seventy-six SBTs but *Starling* and the Group were still in contact.

'The U-boat,' Walker wrote later, 'was sitting pretty well out of reach and all our antics only made him discharge the wretched SBTs. It was all most maddening, but the laugh was very much on our side because not only were asdic conditions perfect and the enemy could easily be held up to a mile, but I could afford to wait for two days while Fritz obviously could not. In any event, it was merely childish of him to try and palm off SBTs on my asdic team and myself. I decided that as he was obviously staying out of reach I would wait until he had either exhausted his patience, his batteries or his high-pressure air.'

By 8 pm Poser had taken several evasive turns quite fruitlessly and attempted to distract his tormentors with more SBTs. But Walker was still in contact, with the remainder of the Group patrolling round two miles away, ready to take over contact should *Starling* lose it.

He told Impey and Burn: 'We will sit it out. I estimate this chap will surface about midnight. Either his air or his batteries will run out by then.'

At two minutes past midnight on June 2nd, the air gave out in *U-202* and Poser ordered: 'Take her to the surface.'

Above, only the faint swish of water round the sloops disturbed the penetrating silence as they waited. Without any audible warning, the U-boat rose fast through the water and surfaced with her bows high in the air where they hung momentarily before falling back into the water. The crew leapt through the conning-tower hatch to man the guns, and Poser shouted for full speed in the hope of outrunning the hunters.

On *Starling*'s bridge, the tiny silver conning-tower and the wash of water were just visible in the moonlight as the U-boat broke surface.

'Starshell ... commence.'

One turret spread the heavens with light, then came the crash and flash of the Group's first broadside laying a barrage of shells round the small target. Through his binoculars, Burn could see a dull red glow leap from behind the conning-tower. The night became alive with flames and tracer bullets streaming towards the stricken U-boat as it twisted violently in the agony of death. A signal lamp blinked from *Starling* and the barrage ceased while Walker increased speed to ram. The ship trembled under increased power, heeled over and rushed towards the riddled enemy now lying stopped and enveloped in coarse red smoke. The range closed and they could see the jagged stump of the conning-tower. Evidently the U-boat was too crippled to escape, so Walker altered course slightly and ran alongside, raking her decks with machine-gun fire and firing a shallow pattern of depth-charges which straddled the submarine and covered her in a cloud of smoke and spray as they rumbled and cracked around her.

When the heaving seas had subsided, she could be seen settling slowly down with waves pouring over her conning-tower and her crew running frantically along the decks, their shouts and screams mingling with the cheers of *Starling*'s own feverishly excited company.

Three high explosive shells had torn great holes in *U-202*'s foredeck, more hits had sliced jaggedly through her conning-tower and fifteen of her crew lay dead or dying at their action stations. Poser clutched the periscope column, pulled a revolver from his pocket and gave his last order.

'Abandon ship ... abandon ship.'

The cry was taken up and passed through the U-boat. Poser turned to say good-bye to his officers. Rather than be captured he was prepared to take his own life. But two of his officers had panicked under the hail of shellfire and, anticipating his order, were already swimming fast from the danger area with a group of sailors who were all crying out for help.

Furiously, Poser threw away his revolver and cursing under his breath decided to be taken prisoner so that one day, when Germany had won the war, he could have the satisfaction of seeing his two defecting officers court-martialled.

By 12.30 am the battle was over and the survivors picked up, two officers and sixteen men in *Starling*, two officers and ten men in *Wild Goose*. The first three to scramble up the nets dangling over *Starling*'s side were stopped when they reached the guard rail and asked the name of their captain and the number of the U-boat. They refused to answer. When this was reported to Walker, he said:

'Don't let them come aboard, Number One. And tell them they cannot be picked up until they have given the information we want.'

The three survivors were ordered back into the water where they shouted and screamed for mercy while Filleul, who was in charge of rescue operations, shrugged and repeated the questions. *Starling* was moving slowly away until one lost his nerve and cried out:

'Kapitan Poser, U-boat *202.*'

He was still sobbing out the reply when they were picked up again, blue with cold. Fifteen minutes later, the scuttling charges in *U-202* exploded and, rolling from side to side, the boat which had escaped destruction within yards of the United States coastline, went to her grace in the middle of the Atlantic. She would break up long before reaching the bottom five miles below.

Later that morning one of Surgeon-Lieutenant Fraser's patients died and Walker ordered a burial at sea with full honours. In his view, he could take any measures he wished to destroy the enemy in as effective a manner as possible and, if Germans lost their lives unnecessarily, they became victims of their own 'total' war. But once the battle was over, he treated prisoners correctly. And a dead German, being also a good one, was entitled to be buried with the ceremony his gallantry deserved.

After the funeral service, *Starling* hoisted the time-honoured signal for a naval victory at sea.

'Second Support Group splice the mainbrace.'

They began moving eastwards on June 5th and finally reached Liverpool four days later. Walker was particularly pleased. His Group was the first to return to harbour with a 'kill'. He had been able to indoctrinate his ships with the team spirit he believed in so passionately and in his own ships he had seen the various fighting departments operate cohesively and efficiently. The guns' crews were especially delighted because both Walker and the First Lieutenant seemed to place more value on the asdic and depth-charges than the guns, which they thought to be noisy gadgets. In fact, both made it only too clear that as anti-submarine experts they considered that depth-charges were the main armament of the ship rather than guns.

This had proved dispiriting to the gunnery team, consisting of the largest number of men in the ship, but the sinking of U-202 had shown that the skill of the asdic operators in holding the target for nearly fifteen hours and the combined depth-charge attacks of the whole Group had not been enough to cripple the enemy. For that, they had been forced to call upon the guns to provide the broadsides.

Eilleen had been told of Johnnie's successes by Captain (D), Liverpool, and wanted to join in the celebrations when the sloops returned to harbour, but three days before their return she was taken to a nursing home for an emergency operation. Within an hour of docking, Johnnie came to her bedside with flowers and a bottle of champagne. Other patients joined them in a toast and the bedside celebration lost nothing of its gaiety.

Meanwhile, Timmy had sailed from Liverpool to join the submarine *Parthian*, then operating in the Mediterranean — fate ironically decreeing that father and son should serve together, one with the hunters and the other with the hunted.

CHAPTER 9: 'CREEPING ATTACK'

Many of the sailors who manned the Second Support Group had never seen action until the night of June 1st/2nd; others had been in action against aircraft only. All had gone into the battle against *U-202* certain that the unseen enemy would strike swiftly and disastrously. Now these fears had been banished forever. An exhilarating keenness to get to grips with the enemy again swept the Group.

Walker's lecture on 'Leadership' earlier that year had included the phrase: 'Don't forget that, in a real emergency, the sailor will always look up to the bridge to see how the skipper is taking it.' Throughout June 1st, the Group had been able to see just that. He had stayed on *Starling*'s bridge for the entire hunt, controlling and directing each attack by signal and loud-hailer. They had seen his grin at every failure; at times they had cursed his unconcern in keeping speeds so low that they were mostly sitting ducks for a torpedo, and they had yearned for a chance to quit the area fast before darkness increased the danger.

Now they identified themselves with Walker. The 'he' had become 'we', and there was something of Walker in every sailor of the Group who strutted confidently ashore in Liverpool taking the greatest pains to ensure that everyone knew he was serving in the Second Support Group.

Nicholas was spending a few days' leave at home and Gillian was expecting to be called up into the Wrens any day. In the mornings, Walker would accompany his wife on various shopping expeditions round Liverpool and spend the rest of the day with Captain (D) and members of the Commander-in-Chief's staff in the Operations Room at Derby House.

In March, it had become apparent that Doenitz was planning a large-scale spring offensive in the Atlantic. This had been greeted sombrely in the House of Commons when Mr Churchill, referring to demands for a Second Front, had stood before the Dispatch Box to warn: 'The defeat of the U-boat must be the prelude to all effective aggressive operations by the Allies.'

By June, Naval Intelligence experts were able to strike a cheerful if cautious note in their secret survey for the first time since the war began.

'Historians of this war,' said the report, 'are likely to single out the months of April and May, 1943, as the critical period during which the strength began to ebb away from the U-boat offensive. For the first time, U-boats failed to press home attacks when favourably placed to do so. Morale and efficiency are delicate and may wither rapidly if no longer nourished by rich success.

'May was black for the U-boats. Sinkings probably averaged nearly one a day.'

In a hurriedly added appendix after a quick analysis of the sinking of *U-202*, the survey continued:

'This hunt, during which continuous contact was held with the U-boat for more than fourteen hours, is a complete vindication of the existing asdic equipment when operated by a well-trained team. The U-boat employed every known tactic while endeavouring to break *Starling*'s contact and fired SBTs regularly, none of which succeeded in misleading the team.'[16]

---

[16] Admiralty Intelligence Surveys.

Following this analysis, the Commander-in-Chief, Sir Max Horton, congratulated Walker on the 'most outstanding performance of the war'.[17]

The Group learned several weeks later that the propaganda departments of Whitehall had not missed the significance of the whittling down of the U-boat offensive. They drew up a leaflet which was dropped in thousands over Germany by Bomber Command, giving an unmistakable message.

> Two thousand U-boat men are now prisoners of war in Britain. But for every prisoner of war, five more U-boat men have died. Life insurance companies in neutral countries estimate the average life of a German U-boat sailor at fifty days. These U-boats have become swimming coffins and now Hitler wants you to join them. If you do, you can look forward to the fastest, and often the most horrible, death in the German armed forces.

It was hoped, perhaps vainly, that this would lead to a marked reluctance on the part of German youth to serve in the U-boat Arm. The German Navy attempted to counter by saying how frightened Britain had become by the U-boat attacks in the Atlantic.

'Germany's enemies,' they announced triumphantly, 'are calling for a Doenitz to combat the U-boat menace. The name Doenitz is a fanfare for the German Navy, but spells terror and horror for the enemy.' But the only 'terror and horror' apparent in Liverpool was the desire of Walker and his Group to sail again as soon as possible.

Derby House and the Admiralty — where new hope was already surging through all levels up to Their Lordships, and from this august body of leaders to the War Cabinet itself —

---

[17] Western Approaches War Diary.

were only too ready to comply with Walker's requests. They divided the Bay of Biscay into two operational areas, code-named 'Musketry' and 'Seaslug', and published an international warning to neutrals to keep their ships clear. It was thought that the Germans might counter by sailing supply ships across the Bay under neutral flags.

Meanwhile, Coastal Command had established daily Sunderland and Catalina flying-boat patrols over the Bay to keep outward bound U-boats submerged, thereby taking longer and using more valuable fuel to reach the Atlantic convoy routes.

These tactics made it imperative to send surface units into the area to hunt and kill the enemy before he could reach the Atlantic deepfield. This would mean close air-sea cooperation, but at least the pilots would know that ships were around to pick up aircrew survivors.

On June 17th, *Starling* led the Group to sea again, bound for 'Musketry', the Biscayan approaches to the principal U-boat bases of Lorient and Bordeaux on the first combined air-sea attempt to bring the battle of the Atlantic to a quick and decisive end by cutting the enemy's operation routes and nailing him to his own doorstep.

The Group — less *Cygnet* which had been transferred to another force — entered 'Musketry' on June 23rd and commenced sweeping southward in line abreast two miles apart at fifteen knots, with *Starling* in the centre. This first day, sunlit and calm, was spent in smoothing out the teething troubles of liaison with Coastal Command. Enthusiastic flying-boat pilots came 'on the air' with reports of U-boats ahead, astern and either side of the Group until Walker was mentally tossing a coin to decide which to chase. These mad dashes around the Bay at full speed revealed old barrels, bits of rotting wreckage and tidal swirls, but no U-boats. It became apparent that aircraft flying high and at the mercy of the wind and weather mistook almost every speck for a U-boat and gave positions which provided the Group navigators with perpetual headaches. One pilot reported himself circling over a U-boat in a position which not only took the Group off their charts but would have landed them miles to the north of Paris. Obviously, there was room for improvement, though for the moment keenness was enough.

In *Starling*, the crew became loudly anti-Coastal Command, with choice selections of descriptive threats of what they would do to those 'ruddy amateurs up there'. By nightfall, the number of false alarms had reduced them to a state of resignation and, unable to stand the clanging alarm bells every few minutes, the crew resigned themselves to the inevitable and slept at their action stations.

At 8 am on the 24th, Walker was in his cabin below the bridge and Filleul was about to take a bath. Six minutes later, the asdic operator reported a definite submarine echo about 1,000 yards ahead accompanied by loud inexplicable whistling noises. The Officer of the Watch called Walker who, after a quick look round, decided to attack without further investigation. He warned the Group by signal to keep clear, and increase speed. Alarm bells brought the crew to readiness and depth-charges were set to explode at 150 and 300 feet.

In the officers' bathroom, Filleul, whose action station was in charge of depth-charges, tied a towel round his waist and rushed to the quarterdeck. Twelve minutes later, *Starling* raced over the attacking position and ten depth-charges exploded in a series of crashing roars in her wake. Subsequent events startled the Group so much that Walker wrote in his Battle Report:

The wretched U-boat surfaced astern with dramatic suddenness as the last roar of the detonating charges died away. For the enemy to surface in the exact spot where the eyes of the whole Group were concentrated, at the first conceivable moment after the pattern was fired, produced such a copybook result that one felt momentarily a sense of disbelief that this was happening.

Their astonishment did not prevent the Group opening up on the enemy with a broadside, and loud, rending crashes punctuated the roar of guns as shell after shell exploded redly against the U-boat's hull. She was still capable of full surface speed, however, and tried to make a run for it. Walker called out to the Yeoman: 'Tell the Group to cease firing. I'm going to ram.'

He ordered full speed and warned the engine room staff to stand by for the impact. At this moment a stray shot from one of the ships exploded against *Starling*'s bows, blowing off the bull-ring — a large circular steel ring through which ropes and wires are fed when tying up in harbour. Walker blinked in some amazement but was concentrating on the enemy. As they drew near, smoke could be seen pouring from the U-boat's conning-tower and she was already seeming to settle in the water. She was still battened down and no attempt was being made to abandon her. For some reason, her captain thought he could still escape.

Starling struck the enemy just abreast the conning-tower. Her bows had risen on a swell and she came down on the U-boat rather than hitting it square. The sloop shuddered under the impact and her crew yelled their cheers as she started to crawl over her victim which could be seen rolling slowly under the keel like some gigantic grey slug.

After the collision, Filleul, the towel flapping about his bare legs, watched the U-boat, upside down with her keel scraping *Starling*'s side, approach the propellers. He ordered a pattern of charges to be set at their shallowest depths and gave the order: FIRE.

They rumbled over the stern and shot from throwers as *Starling* drew clear of the writhing enemy and began to gather speed again. But she was still not quite clear when the charges exploded to give the U-boat her death blow and shatter every light in *Starling*. To make quite sure, *Woodpecker* raced over the same spot still close to *Starling* and gave the U-boat 'one for luck' — a pattern of charges which, had it still been floating, would have smashed it into pieces. There was no hope that anyone could have survived that attack

Walker wrote later:

> I sent *Starling*'s whaler away to collect wreckage and the boat soon produced ample evidence that this particular U-boat had been gathered to his fathers. Locker doors and other floating wreckage marked in German, a burst tin of coffee and some walnuts were soon gathered. My *Starling* had not come through the roughhouse unscathed. The friendly crack on the nose from somebody's gunnery team was taken in good part, but in addition, her beak was bent 30 degrees to starboard, the asdic gone and the for'ard magazines flooded.

One of the Group, taking the blame for knocking off *Starling*'s bull-ring, sent a signal of apology. Walker replied: *No harm done. Just a clout on the snout.*

Wild Goose and *Wren* had meanwhile stumbled across the U-boat's mate and were already pounding him with depth-charges to prevent any attack on the stopped and defenceless *Starling*.

It was by then nearly 10 am and Walker ordered the Group in to attack in turn. *Wren* carried out two attacks, *Woodpecker* followed, then *Wild Goose* and *Kite* finished up. There was no result, and the ships formed up for their next attacks. *Wild Goose* led off and the roar and rumble of crashing depth-charges split the summer's morning as *Kite*, *Woodpecker* and *Wren* followed. Nothing happened and, despite repeated signalled assertions that they were still in contact, Walker was nearly dancing with rage on the bridge of *Starling*.

At one point he astonished his crew by throwing his cap to the deck and stamping on it with impotent fury — mostly pretended — but soon he was grinning again as a new thought struck him. He had absolute confidence in his commanding officers but his love of a good fight was stronger. He ordered the Yeoman: 'Tell the Group to hold the contact and to cease attacking. Then tell *Wild Goose* to stop near me and prepare to exchange commanding officers.'

His excuse was that 'the position was getting out of hand. Ships were getting in each other's way and it appeared they were attacking two separate contacts due, I think, to the presence of SBTs.'

When *Goose* had steered nearly alongside he chatted to Commander Wemyss as though they were at a tea party. 'Want you to take over *Starling*, Dickie, and take her home to Plymouth; she will just about make it. I'll come aboard *Wild Goose* and take command during your absence. Probably meet you in Plymouth. Incidentally, I'm damn sure you chaps have been attacking SBTs.'

The reply was non-committal, as one might expect from a commanding officer who had been interrupted in the middle of a battle and was now being sent home with a ship which might easily sink under him. With one U-boat already making her last plunge to the bottom, another less than a mile away being given a temporary respite in the middle of the Bay of

Biscay known to be alive with U-boats and within range of the enemy's fighter aircraft, Captain Walker was ceremoniously piped over *Starling*'s side as he climbed down a rope ladder into the whaler. The crews of *Wild Goose* and *Starling* lined their decks and cheered wildly as the tiny boat was pulled across the gap to *Wild Goose* with Walker sitting calmly in the stern.

After a few minutes, he was piped aboard *Wild Goose* and Commander Wemyss was being pulled back to *Starling*.

On *Wild Goose*'s bridge Walker muttered 'Good morning' to the officers and men and said: 'Signal the Group: *Let the battle resume. I will pick up contact and direct your attacks.*' He waved across to *Starling* and, as she moved off slowly, signalled: *To … Starling from Captain Walker. Good-bye my gallant Starling. God be with you.*

He found the situation not as out of hand as he had thought. *Wren* was in contact, and Walker reformed the Group for an attack method he had devised while watching the earlier manoeuvres from *Starling*. He now gained contact in *Wild Goose* and ordered the Group to stand by for a 'creeping attack'.

On their hydrophones U-boats could hear the fast revving propellers of an attacker and might take avoiding action. Also, they could hear the asdic impulses on the hulls of their boats and, as these became more rapid, might safely assume that a ship was approaching for an attack. If, however, the asdic impulses were regular the U-boat was likely to believe she was not yet coming under depth-charge attack. Therefore, Walker's plan was to hold contact himself at a range of about 2,000 yards and direct other ships of the Group on to the target at a speed of not more than five knots. This would mean that the U-boat would know nothing about an attack until depth-charges, set to 500 feet and deeper, exploded suddenly around her. However, should a faulty depth-charge detonate too soon the slow-moving ships would be in danger of having their sterns blown off.

Walker pointed *Wild Goose* at the target and called in *Wren* to steam slowly past him under his directions. As she came level, he shouted his instructions over the loudhailer. She was to move directly between himself and the target — 1,000 yards ahead of *Wild Goose* — and proceed dead ahead at five knots. He would instruct her over the R/T, how and when to drop her charges.

Wren crept stealthily into the direct line of attack and moved forward while *Wild Goose* kept the echo at a steady range and bearing. When *Wren* reached the same range and bearing as the U-boat, he called out on R/T: 'Fire a deep pattern and then continue dropping charges set to maximum depth at five-second intervals.'

They watched *Wren* quiver under the impact of the explosions. Nothing came up. The first 'creeping attack' had failed. Walker called up *Kite* and *Woodpecker* and they set off in line abreast for an 'Operation Plaster' barrage attack, dropping more than fifty charges in the next few minutes.

He then ordered *Kite* and *Wren* to approach slowly for another attack. It is doubtful if the U-boat[18] ever knew what hit her. By the wreckage that came bubbling up to the surface it looked as if she must have disintegrated under the blast of the charges from ships she could not have heard coming.

Oil spread over the area, and *Wren* lowered a boat to investigate and pick up evidence of destruction to be forwarded to the Admiralty. It was then nearly 4 pm, and Walker took *Wild Goose* into the centre of the oil to see what they could find in the way of trophies. While leaning over the side of the bridge the sailors nearest to Walker heard a loud

---

[18] Confirmed as *U-449*.

rending noise come from the vicinity of his seat. They burst into scarcely controlled giggles at the large hole that had appeared in his trousers. When he looked round startled and realized what had happened he collapsed in loud laughter. In his report of the action he wrote:

> In my eagerness to view some of the wreckage floating nearby I split, most indecently, the only pair of trousers I had brought with me from *Starling.*

Making little more than eight knots, *Starling* was still in sight. Walker signalled the Group his now familiar 'splice the mainbrace' and detached *Kite* to escort *Starling* back to Plymouth.

The remainder of the patrol is best described by Walker's personal record:

> During the night *Wild Goose*, *Woodpecker* and *Wren* proceeded in line abreast carrying out independent zigzags and searches at twelve knots. After the swift-moving events of the forenoon and a second, if less dramatic success, while the sun was still high, the dark hours produced only an anti-climax. Nothing was seen of a U-boat and if any had been there to provide a hat trick to crown the splendour of this Midsummer's Day, it passed peacefully on its way outside the range of the reduced but no less bloodthirsty Second Support Group.
>
> On June 12th, *Kite* rejoined us, having handed over the safety of my *Starling* to a Hunt class destroyer sent from Plymouth, and immediately reported a periscope. Our hopes stirred but she soon dashed them by amending her report saying the periscope was the horn of a floating mine. Nothing exciting happened in the next two days and we set sail for Plymouth.

Meanwhile, the weather favoured the crippled *Starling* who arrived in Plymouth safely, the shouts and laughter of bathers in front of the Hoe reaching the men lined up on the tilting decks. Some bathers could be seen standing up and shading their eyes as they stared curiously at the odd-looking ship with her flooded bows buried deep in the water and her stern sticking grotesquely into the air. From the Commander-in-Chief's flagstaff ashore flew the signal: *Well done, Second Support Group*.

When at last they tied up alongside a jetty, she was immediately overrun by officials equipped with the largest water pumps they could find, apparently under the impression that *Starling* was about to sink at any minute. The officers led by Filleul, Burn and 'Doc' Fraser headed for the nearest pub. On their return to the jetty, 'Doc' acknowledged the salute of a naval patrol and promptly tripped in a pothole, falling flat on his face. He was the Group's only casualty in the first blockade of the Biscayan ports.

On June 30th, *Wild Goose*, *Wren*, *Woodpecker* and *Kite* entered Plymouth harbour and tied up near *Starling*. From then on the dockyard superintendents were to have the full weight of Walker's rank and energy to have *Starling* ready for sea within a month.

Meanwhile, the First Sea Lord, Commander-in-Chief, Western Approaches, and Commander-in-Chief, Plymouth, had sent signals saying much in few words: *Well done again, Second Support Group*.

At a special conference held by Admiral Sir Charles Forbes in Plymouth, Walker tended to play down the Group's success with the first U-boat.

'This one,' he said, 'really rather deserved its fate. It did not even pay us the compliment of going deep or taking any appreciable avoiding action. I think we must have accidentally caught him with his pants down.'

But, in a letter to the Admiralty, Admiral Forbes said:

'This was the first occasion of a force of British vessels being sent into the Bay of Biscay itself. Much valuable experience was gained and the successes of the Second Support Group have made this strategy undoubtedly worthwhile.'

Starling could look forward to a spell in harbour under repair. Walker was impatient, however, to strike again in the Bay before the enemy could change his tactics. He stayed in *Wild Goose*, leaving Commander Wemyss to supervise the healing of *Starling*'s wounds.

Only three days after returning from the first blockade trip, the Group went to sea for the second time.

CHAPTER 10: 'HOIST GENERAL CHASE'

On July 3rd, 1943, the Group sailed from Plymouth to arrive in the 'Musketry' patrol area the next evening shortly before midnight.

At dawn two days later, a Sunderland reported a U-boat on the surface approximately thirty miles to the west of the Group, and Walker turned at full speed to investigate. Before the ships could arrive at the position, the aircraft reached its Prudent Limit of Endurance and was forced to head for home. It passed over the Group, exchanged signals of mutual regret and vanished into the distance, leaving the sloops with no sign of the enemy. They searched vainly for more than two hours and finally gave up in disgust.

During the morning, a Catalina reported herself attacking three U-boats on the surface and followed quickly with another message saying she had been badly damaged and was returning to base. Her pilot forgot to give any position for the Group to follow up. Another aircraft flew into sight and blinked a signal to Walker saying that mechanical defects made it imperative to return to base.

His departure left the Bay without air patrols of any kind. A biting signal from Walker to Commander-in-Chief, Plymouth about the beauties of air-sea cooperation, when no aircraft were flying, brought immediate results. At noon a Liberator appeared and placed himself under orders. He circled the Group at a range of thirty miles and, for the next few hours, it looked as though an air-sea team had finally been established. Unfortunately, the aircraft could stay only as long as its fuel lasted and, in the early evening, the Group were sorry this cooperative pilot had to fly back to base. Within an hour another Liberator had made a meteoric arrival and disappeared again before Walker could even make contact.

The Group had been steaming eastwards all day and, by nightfall, were only ten miles from the Spanish coast; in fact, their radar screens were showing in clear greenish blobs landmarks known to be fifteen miles inland. The ships about-turned and headed to the northwest corner of 'Musketry', their starting-off point for sweeps towards Bordeaux and Lorient during the next two days.

The series of disappointments continued, and it seemed possible that the enemy had taken steps to counter the blockade. Walker's Report of Proceedings for this voyage reflected some of the frustration felt by the whole Group.

There was something of Drake, Raleigh, Frobisher and Nelson in him. While ashore he was reserved to the point of shyness and restrained in all his dealings with people outside the Service but, once at sea with his own command, swashbuckling tendencies came to the surface. It was impossible for anyone near him not to be affected, and the crew of *Wild Goose*, like the men of *Starling*, soon became inspired with a spirit of dash.

By 11 am they were nearing the reported position of the enemy force and tension mounted when an aircraft reported the sinking of one U-boat. Soon they could see four aircraft circling wildly ahead over a sea covered in a spreading patch of oil. On the fringes were seven disconsolate-looking Germans squatting dumbly in a rubber dinghy. The Group raced past them, Walker signalling to his ships that there was no time to stop and pick them up.

'It will do them no harm to contemplate nature while we do the hunting,' he snapped.

Before *Wren* broke away from the formation, a Liberator dropped a smoke float on a U-boat eight miles away and she was quickly told to resume her station. Walker had turned the Group towards the thin column of smoke when lookouts in all ships sighted a whale blowing indignantly alongside the float. A few derisive signals about 'blind' pilots passed between the ships as they returned to their asdic sweep.

This time *Wren* peeled off and hurried to pick up the Germans, now a tiny speck on the horizon and, at the same time, five JU88s appeared and followed her movements with cautious curiosity while she rescued their countrymen.

U-607, a 50-ton U-boat commanded by Oberleutnant Jeschonneck, had left Lorient for operations off Kingston, Jamaica, on the evening of the 12th. After midnight, champagne had been served to the crew to celebrate the captain's birthday and, for this reason perhaps, they were a little slow in sighting a Sunderland which roared in to attack at 8 am on the 13th. The first bombs scored direct hits on the frantically dodging boat, blowing the conning-tower party into the water. They were the only survivors, the remainder of the crew being trapped in *U-607* which sank immediately.

Jeschonneck and his six companions were swimming together when the Sunderland came low and, for a panic-stricken moment, they feared they were about to be machine-gunned. Instead, the aircraft dropped a raft alongside them and circled high overhead, obviously directing surface units to their position.

By now, even Walker had decided that Doenitz was refusing to give battle and, with this anti-climax, the Group made glumly for Plymouth, which they finally reached on the 16th. Walker found that *Starling* was not yet ready for sea, so he took a few days' leave to see his wife and family in Liverpool and to deliver his Report of Proceedings personally to Sir Max Horton who was demanding first-hand reports of the Group's activities. His obvious delight at Walker's adventures came out in the covering letter he wrote when forwarding the Captain's Official Report to the Director of Anti-Submarine Warfare at the Admiralty.

'This is typical of Walker,' said Sir Max. 'A nice bright and breezy report even if the metaphors are a bit mixed. All huntin', shootin', and fishin' with a little cricket thrown in for good measure.'

By the end of 1942, a large number of ships in the Western Approaches Command had been fitted with new anti-submarine devices designed to reduce the margin of an enemy's potential escape. The asdic was modified to the extent that the operator could not only 'ping' on a target ahead and below but could estimate its depth. Recording machines electrically operated with the asdic set showed a commanding officer roughly what evasive action the enemy was employing. These improved devices called for new armaments for precision attacks. With the 'guesswork' being taken out of the normal attack procedure, it would be possible to fire projectiles to explode on impact.

After the marked lull in June caused by the temporary retirement of the U-boats from the convoy routes, the enemy returned cautiously into the North Atlantic during July. Doenitz threw 150 U-boats into this mid-summer blitz in a concentrated thrust aimed at severing the Atlantic lifelines. To do this, he had to regain the initiative by sending his boats into their patrol areas at the greatest possible speed. This meant sailing across the Bay on the surface and risking losses due to air attack. To minimize the danger, he reverted to sending them out in groups of three, and sometimes five.

When Walker received a copy of this intelligence from Commander-in-Chief, Plymouth, he announced joyfully: 'So they are back on the surface. Long may they continue to be.'

On July 22nd, he transferred his command to *Kite*, handed back *Wild Goose* to Commander Wemyss, welcomed a new sister sloop to the Group — *Woodcock* — and sailed the following day to enforce the blockade in the Bay of Biscay.

When the Second Support Group arrived in the southern section of the Bay for the 'Musketry' patrol at noon on July 25th, he sent the following signal to all ships:

> This time we must deliver a hard enough blow for the Boche to be left in no uncertainty about the fate of his U-boats. He must be made to realize that the Royal Navy considers the Bay of Biscay a happy hunting ground and will stamp out any attempt to restrict the free and rightful passage of Allied shipping. When we meet him we will destroy him. We are a hunting force and from now on, 'a-hunting we will go'.

It was not surprising that from then onwards the famous old song, 'A-Hunting We Will Go', became the Group's signature tune to be played over the leader's loudhailer each time *Starling* entered and left harbour.

During this fine, balmy afternoon with a frivolous sea leaping lightly across the slight, contented swell, the five sloops steered to the southeast towards the coast of Spain in their normal hunting formation, line abreast and two miles apart.

At 6.30 pm they sighted an object which looked to *Kite*'s Officer of the Watch suspiciously like a conning-tower ten miles to port. He sounded action stations, reported to Walker, and the Group turned to investigate. As they drew nearer, the object became a large ocean-going fishing boat and closer inspection proved it to be the Spanish trawler, *Europe 5*, from Vigo. 'Musketry' was one of the areas the Admiralty had promulgated as being used by neutrals at their own risk. Should they ignore the warning and be met by British warships, they were liable to be taken as prize or sunk.

Walker did not hesitate; it was impossible for him to continue his patrol with the trawler in tow as a prize, so he ordered *Wren* to take off the Spaniards and sink her. An hour later, seventeen Spanish fishermen were aboard *Wren*, and *Europe 5* was blown up and sunk.

For the next two days the Group swept to the westward in close contact with air patrols. Walker grumbled that, now air-sea cooperation was working so well that he was rarely without a Sunderland or Catalina in company, the enemy was refusing to give battle. But at noon on the 28th, just as the five ships' companies were being piped to dinner, alarm bells clanged and nearly 1,000 men scrambled to their action stations.

Three more Spanish trawlers had invaded the prohibited area and were about to regret it. Walker instructed *Wild Goose* and *Woodpecker* to take off the crews and destroy the boats while the remainder of the Group covered the operation against enemy intervention. The sea began to fill with trawlers and, in no time, each of the five sloops was busy taking off fishermen and sinking their boats.

The *El Viro* was sunk by *Kite*, *Montenegro* by *Wild Goose*; *Buena Esperansa* by *Woodpecker*; *Don Antonio* by *Woodpecker* and *Comparrel* by *Woodcock*. Another trawler, *H. de Valterra*, was kept in reserve to act as an evacuee ship and, later in the afternoon, all the fishermen, including the seventeen who had enjoyed the hospitality of *Wren* since the 25th, were transferred to her.

This bedraggled little vessel [wrote Captain Walker in his Report] with her decks packed with excited Spaniards, bore some faint resemblance to the old pleasure steamers brought out for the day to cope with the Bank Holiday trippers at home. But she lacked that fleeting air of dignity which befits an old vessel brought out to meet such a situation and, as she lay between *Woodpecker* and *Kite*, she cut a pitiful figure of poverty, neglect and squalor in sharp contrast to the businesslike air of His Majesty's ships and the blue-gold glory of a shimmering afternoon in the Bay of Biscay.

However, carnival gives place to duty and *H. de Valterra* was slapped on the flank and told to go home, which she did to continuous cries of Vive Angleterre' — just as three more trawlers hove in sight. It would, I am sure, be an exaggeration to say that they had heard the buzz and were anxious to join the party. It proved impossible to add them to their gallant band of brothers as the Admiralty had just reported a U-boat in our vicinity, an aircraft had signalled a sighting report and the Group formed up in line abreast and set off to the northwest at full speed.

Nothing came of this search and the Group resumed patrolling through the northwest corner of 'Musketry', their cruise assuming the aspect of peacetime exercises until shortly after 7 am on the 30th when *Wild Goose* intercepted the wireless signals of a U-boat talking to her base at Lorient. Walker wheeled off the Group and set course along the bearing to the southwest and an hour later an aircraft reported himself circling over three U-boats roughly in the same position as that which they were already chasing. By 8.30 am all ships were receiving excellent bearings of the chattering U-boat. She was probably telling Lorient of the aircraft patrolling above herself and her partners. The many and varied positions being signalled by the now wildly excited aircraft were ignored.

147

At 9.30 am the Group sighted an aircraft low on the horizon ahead and almost immediately heard the sound of exploding depth-charges. Alarm bells rang through each ship and the men rushed to their action stations for what looked like an interesting battle.

At 10 am the enemy came in sight on the horizon, three conning-towers turning together to avoid attacks from three aircraft. Four minutes later, Walker's rarely-revealed love of the dramatic came to the fore as he beckoned to *Kite*'s yeoman of signals and ordered: 'Hoist the General Chase.'

For a moment the Yeoman was confused. Then, with a smile of joy, he raced to the rear of the bridge and a few seconds later made a signal used only twice before in the Royal Navy — once by Drake, when he chased the Spanish Armada from the Channel, and again by Nelson when he defeated Napoleon's fleet at the Battle of the Nile. When the flags came down in the executive signal for the order to come into operation, the five sloops surged forward under maximum power, each ship now free to race for the privilege of being the first to engage the enemy. Those with binoculars turned towards *Kite*'s bridge would have seen Walker waving his cap in the air as though, by doing so, he could urge each of his brood on to greater efforts.

The two bloated-looking boats of 1,600 tons, *U-461* commanded by Korvettenkapitan Steibler, and *U-462* commanded by Oberleutnant Bruno Vowe, had sailed from Bordeaux on July 28th for patrols off the Brazilian and central American coasts. Their escort for the Bay crossing was *U-504*, a fast 500-tonner commanded by Kapitanleutnant Luis.

Steibler, a bluff, hearty officer of thirty-six, had only recently brought *U-461* back from North America where he had carried out a special mission for Army Headquarters in Berlin. An Army officer and three civilian wireless specialists had been taken to about fifty miles off the coast of Maine. There they had set up secret radio equipment in the wireless room and locked themselves in. Members of the crew were banned from the room during the operation, but Steibler had known they were using a map of the United States on which all radio stations were marked in red. He could only assume the experts were trying to discover something about these stations.[19]

After lying surfaced for nearly three days, the specialists had completed whatever they were doing and he had headed for home. On the way, he found a lifeboat filled with survivors from the British merchantman, *Teesbank*. He ordered provisions to be passed across and took the merchant skipper, Captain Lorrain, back to Germany as a prisoner.

Nearer France, *U-461* had met the survivors of another British ship, the SS *Saint Margaret*, torpedoed the night before by *U-588*. He took prisoner her captain, Mr D.M.S. Davis of Liverpool, and had more provisions handed down into the lifeboat. Among the survivors were a Polish woman and her daughter and an Englishwoman. Captain Davis called out for someone to tell his wife in Liverpool what had happened, and Steibler set off at full speed on the surface for Bordeaux and the end of an eventful trip.

On the morning of the 30th the three U-boats were making their way westwards on the surface across the Bay when a Sunderland flew out of cloud and began circling them. The Germans were not too worried, being capable of a concentrated combined fire almost guaranteed to scare off the

---

[19] These were actually radar and cypher experts attempting to establish the position of US Coastal and radar stations in preparation for possible commando raids from a U-boat striking force.

most determined pilot. But in the next hour two more aircraft, a Halifax bomber and a United States Liberator, joined the Sunderland and the U-boats could expect a three-cornered attack at any moment.

Steibler was sailing in the centre of the line abreast in formation with Vowe in *U-462* to starboard and Luis in *U-504* to port. The three aircraft roared down to the attack. The first three attempts to dive-bomb were beaten off with a vicious crossfire from the three boats. While they were turning to form up in line ahead, the Liberator came down to bomb *U-504*, now in the lead. With the guns of all three concentrating on this threat, the Sunderland came up astern and dropped a depth-charge neatly alongside *U-461*. It exploded directly underneath her, blowing her vast bulk upwards almost clear of the water. A great hole was torn in her bottom and, as she came down to the surface, the ocean poured into her and she sank in seconds. Only Steibler and fourteen of his crew of sixty survived.[20]

The Sunderland's successful attack — the pilot's first engagement with a U-boat — was made possible only by the Liberator's deliberately diving low to draw the full weight of the enemy fire away from her. It was a gallant gesture and, though badly shot up, O-53 of the United States Army Air Force limped across the Bay and reached Portugal where the pilot made a lucky crash-landing. The crew escaped injury and were later returned to the United Kingdom by the Portuguese authorities.

When the range closed to six miles the Second Support Group, with *Kite* slightly in the lead and Walker waving his cap

---

[20] By a curious coincidence the identification number of the Sunderland which sank was also *U-461* — denoting it was aircraft 'U' of 461 Squadron.

and grinning to the next ship in line, opened fire with their for'ard guns. The battle now became a strictly naval occasion and the aircraft withdrew to watch the Group race into action, guns roaring, engines pulsating and bow waves high as they drove through the choppy seas.

A Royal Air Force officer wrote later: 'It was a grand sight, those five ships in line abreast cutting along at full speed in a blue-white sea under a deep-blue sky. The guns roared and the smell of cordite hung over the ocean and guns' crews cheered as shells dropped near the twisting targets.'

On the conning-tower of *U-462*, Vowe, an elderly officer promoted from the lower deck, was feeling anxious. His boat had been hit by three shells, badly holed and two of his officers were suffering from wounds caused by shell and splinters. There seemed little likelihood of making a surface escape with five ships on his heels. As the next barrage screamed overhead, he ordered scuttling charges to be set. The shells were dropping close again. There was a stunning explosion on the foredeck as two hits exploded in quick succession. To stay aboard any longer would be suicide. Vowe shouted his next order: 'Abandon ship.'

Within a few minutes the crew were swimming in the water and, as the scuttling charges went off, the stricken U-boat shuddered under the impact of more direct hits. Then she caved inwards and sank.

On the bridge of *Kite*, a signalman read a message being flashed from the Halifax bomber. *Congratulations, U-boat no more.*

With both 'milch cows' sunk, there remained the operational escort, *U-504*. A worried witness of the fate which had overcome his two brothers-in-arms, Kapitanleutnant Luis had not waited for the gunfire barrage of the Group to be turned on him. He dived and went deep in the hope of escaping under cover of the confusion caused by survivors and wreckage on the surface. He reckoned without Captain Walker who, guessing his intentions, formed the Group in circles patrolling round the spreading oil, wreckage and survivors. In less than five minutes, *Kite* gained asdic contact and Walker ordered an immediate attack.

It took him a few minutes to reach this decision; the point of attack would be less than half a mile from where the shouting survivors were swimming in clusters. Later he wrote in his Report:

> When I ordered *Kite* into attack no one could foretell what effect it would have on the members of the Aryan bathing party who were but a short distance astern with the whites of their eyes clearly visible. It was a fateful moment although there was no question of a sword hanging over their heads; rather was their fate to be decided much lower down.

Contact with the U-boat was lost and regained intermittently until 11.30 am when Walker withdrew the Group to take stock of the situation. There was no doubt that the U-boat had gone deep after the first attack. It was now necessary, in his view, to 'get down to the job seriously'.

Placing *Kite* in position as the directing ship, he lined up the Group for a series of creeping attacks alternated with three-ship barrage assaults. *Woodpecker* crept in silently to drop twenty-two depth-charges at maximum settings. *Wild Goose* followed. It was enough. Oil and wreckage plummeted to the surface, including planks of wood, a mass of sodden clothing, a side of bacon and a human lung.

'The bacon had been well cured,' wrote Walker grimly, 'but the lung was very new.'

With *U-504* and the hopeful Kapitanleutnant Luis destroyed, the Group returned to the bunches of survivors who were distributed between *Kite*, *Wren* and *Woodpecker*.

That evening they sighted a yellow sail and Walker ordered *Woodpecker* to pick up the occupants of the raft. These were found to be the crew of a Focke-Wulf which, they said, had been shot down by a Beaufighter on July 29th. However, *Woodpecker*'s doctor reported that two of the wounded survivors had received their injuries not later than the 27th. This caused some puzzlement among the Group as no one could imagine why the Germans should bother to lie about a harmless date.

By the 31st, the Group had reached 'U-boat Alley', the direct route across the Bay between the Atlantic and Bordeaux and begun sweeping towards the French coast. At 9 am on August 1st, another eventful day for the Second Support Group opened with the report of an aircraft that she was circling a U-boat riding fast on the surface towards open sea only forty miles away.

For two hours they crashed along at full speed through rough seas and a short heavy swell with no further report from the aircraft. A Catalina then came in sight to give the position of a U-boat on the surface which was almost certainly that reported earlier. This aircraft proved an attentive and efficient guide. He had dropped a smoke float on the spot where the U-boat had dived and proceeded to con the Group to the marker.

Walker commenced his sweep steering westwards in the belief that the U-boat would continue on her passage to the Atlantic and, shortly after 2 pm, his lookouts sighted a Sunderland bombing a target ten miles ahead. The Group raced forward and were closing the U-boat rapidly when the Sunderland made another attack. To the horror of the watching sailors, the aircraft failed to pull out of her dive and crashed headlong into the sea. There came a deafening roar as her remaining bombs exploded. It seemed impossible that anyone could have survived.

When the Group raced up, they found six RAF men safe in a makeshift raft while, farther away, crouched the terrified crew of the destroyed U-boat. The crews of all five ships cheered in spontaneous admiration for an aircraft which had pressed home its attack in the face of such a hot barrage from the enemy that both pilots had been killed — but not before their bombs had gone on their way to kill the U-boat.

This was *U-454*, commanded by Kapitanleutnant Backlander, a man who struck the officers of *Kite* as being that rare breed, a pleasant type of non-political German. Only twelve others of his crew of forty-five survived. *Wren* was detached to pick up the RAF crew who were using a wing of their broken aircraft as a raft.

On August 2nd, the day began with reports that a force of enemy Narvik-class destroyers had sailed from the French ports to clear the Bay of the Second Support Group. This caused Walker to order the Group into line-ahead formation and steer at full speed for the French coast to engage the enemy. As this class of destroyers were virtually young cruisers, some in the Group thought that their Leader was taking a bite at something a little too big this time. The vast majority, however, were sublimely confident. Guns were cleared for action in an atmosphere of cheerful anticipation of a new and bigger kill.

The Group hunted for the German force for two days without success and were eventually ordered to return to Plymouth, where they arrived on the 6th. At the flagstaff in front of Admiralty House, the C-in-C's residence, flew the signal: *Well done again, Second Support Group*.

Walker, who had fired depth-charges when men were in the water nearby, had killed more Germans than any other officer in the Western Approaches Command, felt keenly that the Spanish fishermen operating in the 'Musketry' area were unaware that they invited instant death by their fishing in prohibited waters. As soon as *Kite* had been tied up alongside, he made his way ashore and reported to the Commander-in-Chief's staff:

'I feel it should be widely promulgated that these Spaniards are a harmless, ignorant and cheerful lot, utterly pro-British. It is unlikely that the order to attack on sight in "Musketry" could ever be carried out by a British naval officer who was aware of this.'

As a result, the Admiralty amended its shoot-to-kill order for the blockade, instructing instead that Spanish fishermen should receive the sort of treatment given them by the Second Support Group — evacuation from their ships, which should then be sunk, and sent back to Spain in a refugee trawler kept afloat for the purpose.

To Walker's joy, *Starling* had completed her refit, carried out trials and was ready for duty. Handing *Kite* to her commanding officer, he transferred back to his old quarters in *Starling*.

On arrival in harbour, he telephoned Eilleen to join him in Plymouth where she arrived in time to see the German prisoners marched into captivity. They had a week-end together before Johnnie sailed again, leaving his wife to stay for a short holiday with some friends in Somerset before returning to Liverpool. While there she received her first warning that something had happened to Timmy.

A letter was forwarded to her from a friend of her son's. It offered condolences on his death. Deeply shocked, Eilleen wrote to Captain (D), Liverpool, asking if he could find out if the submarine *Parthian* were all right. Several days of anxious, agonizing hopes punctuated by moments of depression followed until eventually she cut her holiday short and returned to Liverpool. At home there was a message asking her to telephone Captain (D) and intuitively she realized that the letter-writer had known the truth. On calling Captain (D)'s office she learned that *Parthian* was overdue and presumed lost from an operation in the Mediterranean. It was thought at Derby House that the Group would return to Liverpool the following week. Eilleen requested that her husband should not be told the news while at sea.

Meanwhile the Group, which had sailed on the 9th, was now engaged in a battle with the Luftwaffe.

CHAPTER 11: SECRET WEAPONS

During July, the blockade of the Bay of Biscay began to yield results; twenty-one U-boats were sunk by air and sea patrols in the 'Musketry' and 'Seaslug' areas, sightings were fewer and it seemed that Doenitz was exploring a possible alternative route to the Atlantic by sailing his boats down the Spanish coast inside the three-mile territorial waters limit.

Interrogation of survivors had begun to show a deterioration in the U-boat crews. The Intelligence survey for July, 1943, said:

> Main reasons for the decline in morale are the heavy U-boat losses and a growing realization that Germany can no longer hope to win the war. At least two out of every five prisoners are quite willing to admit that they have had more than enough of the war which they consider as good as lost. Their own war-weariness is increased by depressing letters from equally tired relations and friends inside Germany.

Doenitz's attempts to find a route round the Bay instead of across it became apparent when the Second Support Group arrived for their next patrol in the 'Musketry' area on August 12th. There were few aircraft sightings of the enemy and, throughout the patrol, the Group enlivened proceedings by a series of encounters with the Luftwaffe.

On the first day they sighted a party of eight JU88s who darted in close for a quick look before making off at high speed. The next day another flock paid a brief visit and, in the afternoon, the ships sighted an empty RAF rubber dinghy half-submerged. In the evening, the sloops were in sight of the

Spanish coast when nine JU88 fighter-bombers circled above and looked as though they were about to attack. Action stations were sounded and, as the aircraft came in low on the horizon, they were met by a full barrage from the six sloops, followed by a stream of machine-gun and Oerlikon tracers which forced them to swerve away and split up.

It was not Walker's way to take evasive action; he forced the Group into line abreast and at full speed headed towards the regrouping point of the aircraft over the Spanish coast; a gesture more of bravado than menace. Enemy planes screamed in low again, but this time Walker kept his armament silent, allowing the aircraft to come into range of the small-arms before giving the executive signal to open fire. The JU88s were caught in a fierce fan of gunfire which again they were unable to penetrate; instead they broke away, two of them heading back towards France with smoke belching from their tails.

By this time, almost a revolution in air-sea warfare had taken place. In effect, six sloops doing twenty-one knots were chasing a formation of aircraft capable of more than 300 miles an hour. The enemy carried out the next attack in two groups — one of three and the other of four — at a great height. They were greeted by a barrage from eighteen twin-barrelled mountings which split up their formations and sent them scattering back to the coast. Another plane was seen to be in difficulty, losing height as it changed course and headed northwards from the battlefield. This was their last attempt. They circled out of range while the ships, reaching the three-mile limit of Spanish waters, turned on a sweep towards Bordeaux. Only then did the remaining six aircraft vanish into the haze, chased and defeated by surface units.

It was a remarkable encounter. Although no planes were seen to crash — and therefore could not be claimed — it is certain that two and probably three were damaged without ever dropping a bomb or firing a shot. The sloops were fortunate perhaps that the aircraft had not been led by a more determined leader.

On the 10th, three Focke-Wulf bombers came accidentally within range of the Group's guns and were chased away with shells exploding around them. Four days later the sloops headed for Liverpool having neither sighted nor gained contact with anything more exciting than a school of porpoise.

In fact, the success of the Second Support Group in 'Musketry', of other Groups patrolling in 'Seaslug', and of Coastal Command and patrols supported recently by Mosquito squadrons to ward off marauding JU88s, enforced the blockade to the extent that Doenitz had lost the initiative for the first time since the fall of France and the occupation of the Biscayan ports.

In deference to Eilleen's wishes Johnnie had not been told about the fate of *Parthian*. Now, when the Group were about to enter Gladstone Docks, she prepared to meet him and break the news quietly in the privacy of his cabin. But while *Starling* was being manoeuvred into position for the tricky approach to the narrow entrance of the dock, a signalman reported to Walker:

'There is someone ashore waving as though he wants to come aboard urgently, Sir.'

It was an officer from Derby House and, as *Starling* nosed her way through the entrance, he leapt on to the quarterdeck and rushed up to the bridge. After saluting, he said:

'I have been ordered to report to you, Sir, that your son Timothy is believed to have been killed in action while serving in the submarine *Parthian*.'

A shocked silence followed his words; with the seeming exception of Walker, all were stunned by the news and the almost indecent haste with which it had been given, not through any fault of the officer, but because no one had waited until the ship was safely docked.

Walker's face was expressionless as he continued to bring *Starling* alongside the jetty. It was a difficult manoeuvre at the best of times and Walker, superb seaman as he was, could not lay claim to being an expert ship handler in confined waters. This time, he conned his ship brilliantly and, after 'Finished with Engines' had been rung on the telegraph, left the bridge without a word to greet Eilleen at the gangway and escort her to his cabin.

Starling's officers helped them both through that difficult morning. One by one they came to their Captain's cabin to have a drink and try to talk light-hearted nonsense. Eilleen still remembers how much it meant not to have a procession of people coming to offer sympathy.

In the afternoon, they visited the Red Cross headquarters in Liverpool to register Timothy's biographical details on the chance that he might still be alive and taken prisoner. In their own hearts, however, they realized he was dead, although the Admiralty officially recognized him at this stage as being missing.

By an earlier arrangement, *Starling's* Wardroom were giving a party the next afternoon for the officials and wives of a borough which had more or less adopted *Starling*, Filleul offered to have the party cancelled, but neither Johnnie nor Eilleen would hear of it. The party was held as arranged and even the hosts seemed to be enjoying it. No mention was made of the tragic blow under which Captain and Mrs Walker were suffering until someone, looking at the family photographs in

Johnnie's cabin, asked Eilleen how many children she had. Unthinkingly she answered four … then she stopped short in sudden realization, her eyes meeting her husband's across the cabin. The incident was passed over in a spate of chatter.

It has since been suggested in various newspaper reports that Captain Walker fought from that time onwards in a spirit of revenge. This was not so; he hated the Nazi creed and would take any measures to stamp it out. But towards the Germans as people he was completely impersonal — they were foreigners he hardly knew.

During this period in harbour, the *London Gazette* published a list of awards to the Second Support Group for their exploits on the 'Musketry' patrols. In his Reports of Proceedings, Walker took care to recommend those officers and ratings he thought had done what he called a 'good job of work'. Conversely, he would always stress tactical blunders for which he considered himself responsible. The *Gazette* was a sure guide to the opinions of his senior officers ashore. He was made a Commander of the Order of the Bath — only officers of Flag Rank were made Knights — and once again the citation stressed, among other qualities, his skill in leadership.

Starling's First Lieutenant and asdic officer, Lieutenant Impey, had already received a DSC while serving under Walker in *Stork*. Now he received the DSO but, before the ships sailed again, contracted an illness which put him ashore indefinitely. Filleul found he had been given a double honour — the DSC and, at Walker's invitation, he replaced Impey as First Lieutenant. The communications team were not forgotten. Yeoman of Signals E. C. Keyworth and Chief Petty Officer (Telegraphist) T. Teece, already the holders of the DSM, both received Bars.

On the second evening ashore, John and Wendy Filleul were invited with Alan Burn to dine with the Walkers at 'The White House'. Eilleen had recovered from her illness and, to her husband's obvious relief, seemed in cheerful spirits. Gillian and Wendy had both joined the Wrens, so the dinner was an all-naval occasion. Walker, the host, was courteous and flattering. To the amazement of his young officers, who were accustomed only to taking his orders and admiring him from a respectful distance, he waited on them with an old-world dignity, personally seeing that they had everything they wanted and not allowing his wife to carry the brunt of Guest Night. It is for such simple gestures that Walker is remembered today by his old officers.

Towards the end of August, Doenitz resumed his offensive against the North American coastal and Atlantic convoy routes; on the 31st, *Starling* led the Group to sea again — less *Woodpecker* which had gone to Bristol for a refit. They carried out a series of anti-submarine exercises off Londonderry and set course for the Bay of Biscay on September 6th.

Approaching 'Musketry' they came across a small sailing vessel which turned out to be the French fisherman *Nana Goutreau*, from La Rochelle. According to Captain Walker's report:

> No vessel afloat could have conveyed to the most suspicious observer a more peaceful or innocuous impression and this little vessel's inoffensive appearance was not belied by my boarding party.
>
> However, a striking force patrol in the Bay has no time to enthuse over the beauty of sail or the ancient calling of fishermen, so after her crew had been taken aboard *Woodcock* she was scuttled at noon on September 8th. She went down

with her mainsail still set and her outsize fishing rods waving plaintively in the air against the sky. This was the nearest the Second Support Group had ever come to shooting an albatross.

At dawn next morning, the Group sighted a dinghy tossing dangerously in a choppy sea and heavy swell. In it were five survivors from the crew of a Liberator which had been attacked by four JU88s eight days before. The bomber had destroyed one enemy plane before being shot down herself, with the pilot and sergeant co-pilot dead at the controls.

Shortly after the remainder of the crew had taken to the dinghy, a U-boat surfaced alongside. The aircrew asked the Germans for some drinking water — to be needed badly in the days ahead — but, in Captain Walker's own words: 'This simple request from a beaten adversary was refused by the gallant U-boat captain in accordance with the accepted traditions of the U-boat Arm.'

Only a few hours before being picked up by *Wild Goose*, two more officers in the dinghy had died of exposure and thirst. Another, a Sergeant Bareham, was seriously wounded and in spite of continuous medical treatment died on September 10th. Seven hours later, Pilot Officer Collins also died of exposure and exhaustion. They were buried at sea from *Wild Goose* the same day.

That evening a signal was received from Commander-in-Chief, Western Approaches, ordering two of the Group to the assistance of a North Atlantic convoy, XE11. Walker detached *Kite* and *Woodcock*, while the remaining three sloops continued their patrol to the south.

At 2.20 pm on the 15th, five JU88s were sighted flying out of range down the starboard side of the Group and twenty minutes later eight more appeared. This long, thin enemy

163

procession flew completely round the Group, and Walker saw it as a curtain-raiser for more evil events.

At 3 pm a Halifax bomber rushed to the scene and stayed close to the Group for the next three hours, obviously seeking protection under their guns. His vast bulk tempted four of what were thought to be enemy planes to attempt a quick thrust low over the water. The Group opened fire but stopped after the first salvo when the 'marauders' were recognized as Mosquitos, apparently nothing to do with the patrolling JU88s and wanting no part of them. They swished over the sloops and vanished towards the coast of France.

The next arrival, in the early evening, was a Liberator which came and went abruptly before they had time to establish signalling contact. All this coming and going of friends and enemies kept the interest of the sloops at a high pitch, Walker's most of all. He wrote later:

> It is probably a great many years since most of the officers in *Starling* had read *Alice in Wonderland*, but a child of twelve would have had no difficulty in explaining what this great scurrying to and fro brought to mind. All these events seemed to be working up to an Imperial Tea Party indeed, but it is reported regretfully that after all the preparations that had been made by the Group nothing happened for the remainder of the day.

> For the next two days they patrolled about 100 miles off Bordeaux and down to Spanish territorial limits. Early on the morning of the 17th it was reported that a British aircraft had been shot down about seventy miles to the north, and the sloops set off to search for survivors. The report and the Group's navigation proved satisfyingly accurate when at 8 am they sighted a dinghy; half an hour later eleven of a crashed Sunderland's aircrew were sipping hot cocoa aboard *Starling*, By coincidence, the captain of the aircraft and six members of

the crew had been in the Sunderland which had destroyed the *U-461*, at the time when the Group had raced across the Bay under the 'General Chase'.

Later that day, *Kite* and *Woodcock* rejoined, having had an adventurous twenty-four hours assisting XE11 through a danger area. At one time the two sloops had sailed into the outfield to meet a formation of JU88s flying in low to attack the convoy. The aircraft were met by the combined fire of the ships and, after a thirty-minute engagement in which neither side scored hits, the enemy broke off the action without getting nearer to their main target.

The Group returned to Liverpool on the 20th with fourteen airmen and four French tunnymen — the latter, if anything, more excited at their adventure and the prospect of being guests of the British Government than the RAF men returning to fly again.

Between May and August, the U-boat Arm had taken a severe beating. In the Bay, Coastal Command aircraft and the Second Support Group had made the passage en route to the Atlantic a dangerous undertaking; on the northern Atlantic convoy routes, increased escort groups operating under continuous air cover were taking a heavy toll of the 'packs'. The stamina and efficiency of the U-boat crews began to wilt and when they returned to harbour there was no rest, for the Allied offensive was maintained by nightly visits to the Biscayan bases by Bomber Command.

By August Admiralty Intelligence could report: 'The U-boats have been forced on the defensive and for the moment appear to have no antidote for the great and growing power of the Allies working together in unison on the sea and in the air.'

This was unusually encouraging from a source which preferred to survey the Atlantic scene cautiously; and it gave rise to the premature hope that, if the battle were not yet won, victory was at least in sight. Doenitz, probably the finest U-boat tactician Germany had ever produced, made a practice of probing our defences and striking hard when a weak link was exposed in the thin chain stretching over the vast, lonely wastelands of the north and south Atlantic. By the time we had raced reinforcements to one area he had found a crack elsewhere. Late in August, he discovered that Allied convoys from America to North Africa were being routed for speed 500 miles southwest of the Azores — an area which shore-based aircraft could not reach — and returned to the offensive in two directions.

He spread more than a hundred U-boats across the Atlantic — some to cut the smaller supply arteries off Rio de Janeiro, Freetown, Mexico and the West Indies, while his main forces were concentrated in the 'Black Hole' to intercept convoys taking the southern route to the Mediterranean and again along the northern routes to disrupt the supplies of men and materials gathered in Britain for the invasion of Normandy.

This offensive was accompanied by the introduction into the Battle of the Atlantic of two new weapons which struck a sombre chord in the wearied breasts of our sailors who were faced yet again with the spectre of U-boat supremacy and the mass destruction of convoys.

The first of these 'secret weapons' made its appearance on September 20th when two west-bound convoys, one of nearly fifty ships and the other of some thirty-odd, both with escorts, were within ninety miles of each other nearly 700 miles out into the Atlantic. Long-range air cover was supplied by Liberators from Iceland, and twenty U-boats were known to be operating in the vicinity.

At dawn, one of the escorts was torpedoed, losing her stern, and soon afterwards the two merchant ships nearest to her were also torpedoed. One of the escorts took the stricken warship in tow, and miraculously she made port, barely afloat.

Meanwhile, the two convoys joined forces at noon and pooled their escorts — an operation easier to order than effect. Nearly 100 merchant ships had to be re-organized without loss of speed by a handful of escorts. The senior officer of the combined escort group, Commander (now Captain) M. J. Evans, wrote later: 'The two convoys gyrated majestically round the ocean, never appearing to get much closer to a union and watched appreciatively by a growing swarm of U-boats.'

The combined convoy was seven miles deep and eight miles across when the first attacks developed after dark. For the next five nights, sometimes in dense fog, they were under continuous assault and eventually reached safety on the sixth day — at a price. Despite the strain of handling so many ships in fog while knowing that the U-boat 'packs' were in contact by hydrophones, only six merchant ships were lost. Far more serious was the loss of three warships and another damaged, for the probable destruction of three U-boats. Curiously, all the warships torpedoed had reported their sterns blown off.

An intense interrogation began of the crew of the one that made port under tow to find the answer to this curious phenomenon. This inquiry, followed by an analysis of the escort's manoeuvring at the time she was hit, when added to the reports of the three warships which had been sunk, reached an astonishing and alarming conclusion. The enemy was apparently using a torpedo which followed a ship's course and struck her in the stern. Intelligence soon provided indisputable evidence that Doenitz was equipping his U-boats with three or four of these acoustic weapons, and the true picture began to unfold.

This deadly torpedo was intended primarily to destroy escorts so that a convoy would be left unprotected at the mercy of ordinary torpedoes. The new weapon could be fired at extreme range in the general direction of an escort. It would then 'hear' her propellers and automatically alter course towards the target, faithfully following her zigzags until hitting the propellers and blowing off her stern. This provided a disquieting thought to depth-charge crews whose action station was on quarterdecks.

Only experience in action would produce a countermeasure; meanwhile, morale among the escorts of the Western Approaches Command took a serious knock. What could be done about torpedoes which followed you around until they hit?

The second weapon made its appearance in the battle late in September while the Second Support Group, still without *Woodpecker*, was patrolling off Lorient searching for U-boats which continued to creep across the Bay surfacing only at night for the minimum time necessary to charge their batteries.

They saw nothing on this patrol, although on September 29th a signal was received warning all ships of an air attack in which an escort had been subjected to a 'glider bomb' assault. A Dornier bomber was apparently sighted by this escort off the French coast and it cautiously circled out of range. Surprisingly, it flew towards the escort as though to attack but, while still at extreme range, let go a missile which looked like an ordinary bomb with miniature wings. Instead of falling, the bomb headed direct for the startled ship. Before reaching its target, the bomb executed a tight turn and dived into the sea.

When the Group returned to Liverpool on October 9th, they studied reports of the incident and learned that the bomb was the first guided missile ever to be launched in anger. It was rocket-propelled, fitted with small wings to give stability, and radio-controlled on to its target from the launching 'parent' aircraft.

Morale was shaken again. Not only were the escorts to be chased by 'gnats', as the acoustic torpedoes were nicknamed, but now they could be attacked from the air with bombs directed on to them no matter what evasive action they employed. The men of Western Approaches dubbed the glider bombs, 'Chase-me-Charlies'.

From the 'gnat', Admiralty experts established some measure of defence. If escorts steamed at not more than eight knots or not less than twenty-four they were immune. Analyses of widespread attacks showed that the torpedoes were hard to shake off between these speeds, but could not 'hear' propellers outside them. There was an important snag. At seven knots the escort would be too slow for the convoys, and at twenty-five the convoys would be too slow for the escorts.

Another defence was the introduction of 'foxers' — a device which would, it was hopefully supposed, attract the 'gnat' and explode it well astern of the target. This consisted of a series of wires trailed over the stern on the end of which were long strips of metal. When a ship was at sea, according to theory, the metal strips were tossed around in the wake some fifty yards astern and clashed together, making a din the 'gnats' could not fail to hear above the noise of the propellers. Walker had no use for the 'foxer'. It made so much noise the asdic set became practically useless. He rarely used it, relying instead on contacting the enemy first.

Against the 'Chase-me-Charlies' there was no defence until, one day in the Bay, an escort was attacked by an aircraft which launched its 'glider bomb' just as a scientist aboard switched on his electric razor to test out a theory. To the amazement of the ship and the enemy aircraft, the new weapon gyrated about the sky in a fantastic exhibition of aerobatics, finally giving chase to its own 'parent'. In some inexplicable way, the 'Chase-me-Charlie' control system had been affected by electric waves given off by the razor. This method was never officially admitted by the Admiralty as a defence measure, but the ships which sailed into the 'Chase-me-Charlie' areas found it foolproof. In Liverpool there was a sudden run on shops selling all makes of electric razors.

In October, it became apparent that Doenitz had switched tactics again and was launching his autumn offensive against the north Atlantic convoy routes in a sustained effort to curtail the invasion build-up. With the 'gnats' taking their toll of our escorts, and a new threat growing against the major convoys, it was decided to make the mid-Atlantic 'Chop' Line area our first line of defence. American forces continued to operate south of the Azores, while the Royal Navy undertook to send carriers north of the islands. The Biscayan blockade had proved successful. The enemy in transit had been tamed and, for the moment, Coastal Command could forestall any attempts at a mass break-out.

The Second Support Group went into training for the north Atlantic — without *Starling*.

Walker approved of exercises, theoretical training and commanding officers' courses for all his captains but not himself. Stubbornly he refused to spend long days at Tobermory, considered by many as the cradle of victory in the Atlantic, but encouraged his captains to take every opportunity to go there. He resisted for himself the introduction of new methods to deal with U-boats devised to coordinate the latest weapons and equipment.

If this appeared as autocratic vanity, it was certainly not baseless. With his 'bow-and-arrow' unmodified asdic he had destroyed more U-boats and killed more Germans than any other commander in the Navy. He had a gift for 'smelling out' the enemy, and his mind could unravel the tactical problems of attack as quickly and accurately as any machine. He instructed his captains to exercise and train in the orthodox manner providing that, once at sea, they forgot temporarily what they had learned and reverted to *his* way of doing things.

This stubborn attitude became manifest when Captain (D), Liverpool, suggested he should visit the Tactical Training School set up to train commanding officers and asdic teams in dealing with the various evasive actions a U-boat might take when under attack. It was a sound course considered to be excellent value by most Western Approaches captains. Walker was quite willing to agree, but firmly rejected any proposal that he himself should attend the school. A staff officer told him that Sir Max Horton was taking a poor view of this dogmatic attitude but Walker stuck to his guns.

It is a striking commentary on his reputation and prestige that he could get away with it. Although the most senior ranking officer afloat in the Western Approaches Command, he should still have carried out the general orders governing the working-up, training and equipping of all ships. Somehow, none seemed able to pin him down and he managed to elude issues of this kind without ever openly disobeying orders.

While the Group trained at Tobermory until October 14th, and *Starling*'s officers attended courses at the Tactical Training School and drilled their crews, Walker pottered in his garden at home, went shopping with Eilleen and romped with Andrew in the evenings.

His paper work as a captain had so piled up in *Starling* that someone was clearly needed to administer the whole Group's office and confidential report work. Captain (D), Liverpool, was persuaded to part with one of his secretarial staff, Lieutenant H. W. F. (Bill) Johnson, RNVR, who became Walker's secretary and personal assistant.

So far there had been no chance to try out the various defences against the 'gnat' and the 'Chase-me-Charlie'. For the latter nothing really effective had been devised as too little was known about it. It was decided that a striking force should sail under specific orders to test out the varying-speeds theory and 'foxer' device against 'gnats' and to encourage a 'Chase-me-Charlie' attack in the hope of shooting one down to be brought home for examination.

The selected force would have to be capable of long-range anti-aircraft fire, for the real menace of the 'Chase-me-Charlie' lay in the relatively poor anti-aircraft armament in the majority of escort vessels. Corvettes, frigates and destroyers built in the United States for service in the Atlantic under the White Ensign were designed to beat the U-boat but not aircraft as well. These warships had no way of tackling aircraft which fired and controlled rocket-bombs.

The double task of acting as guinea pigs and experimental ships fell to the Second Support Group whose powerful guns, high speed and general design made them ideal opponents for the 'Chase-me-Charlies'.

On October 15th, Walker had the crew of *Starling* mustered on the quarterdeck.

'Our main job,' he said, 'is to seek out the U-boats and destroy them. If in doing so, we can persuade them to fire off a few of their 'gnats' all the better. We shall then find out if these damned awkward "foxers" really work.' He grinned at the blur of faces. 'Don't worry. The Boche hasn't managed to think up anything we can't beat yet. Once we get even a smell of him I shall reduce speed to below seven knots and hunt him down.

'But about these "Chase-me-Charlies". There's only one thing we can do. You gunnery boys who are always complaining that I do not show a proper respect for your toys will have a chance to show how good you really are. All you have to do is shoot the things down. Simple enough if you remember that if you don't they are very liable to hit us.'

Smilingly, he told the First Lieutenant to 'carry on' and strode away. In the afternoon, *Starling* sailed to rendezvous off Londonderry with the rest of the Group and the aircraft-carrier *Tracker*, for their first hunting strike into the mid-Atlantic wastelands. *Kite* was in Londonderry repairing minor damage caused in a collision with a tug, and would catch up later; *Woodcock* was still at Bristol and *Wren* at the Clyde having new equipment fitted. To compensate, a new sloop called *Magpie*[21] had joined the Group.

By nightfall they were on their way to take the sting out of the scorpion's tail.

---

[21] This ship later became the first command of the Duke of Edinburgh, then Lieutenant Mountbatten, RN.

CHAPTER 12: ATTACK BEFORE BREAKFAST

The striking force swept into the Atlantic with the sloops drawn up in line abreast ahead of the aircraft-carrier which zigzagged independently a mile astern. On October 19th, they ran into filthy weather — driving wind, rain, hail and sleet, high turbulent seas, and a menacing roller-coaster swell which tossed the smaller ships about until all movement on their decks had to be stopped. This meant that those aft stayed there and those forward handled the bridge and gun watches without relief.

The sky was black with heavy, rain-laden cloud racing low across the water reducing visibility to less than a mile. Life in *Starling* was wretched; men drenched by spray and rain went below to the mess decks only to find cracked rivets letting in thin drips of water over their bunks and mess tables. Walker's own cabin below the bridge became a swilling mess of dirty water as bulkheads sprung leaks round his bunk and in the dockhead. The plating of the quarterdeck cracked, and a large gap let water flow freely into the wardroom, while the whole stern began to quiver and move about independently of the rest of the ship, like a dog wagging its tail, threatening serious damage to the propeller shafts.

In the gloom of dawn next day Walker ordered speed for the force to be reduced to eight knots. Behind the sloops, *Tracker* wallowed and heaved like a huge elephant in agony. Her damage repaired, *Kite* rejoined, having battled against the storm to catch up and in so doing suffered more damage than had been inflicted by the tug.

Midday was more like midnight, and dusk as black as the inside of a bat, but early on the 22nd the storm seemed to be ending and the Commander-in-Chief, Western Approaches, ordered Walker to alter course to support the westbound convoy ON27, already under close escort and supported by Commander Gretton's famous B7 Group in company with the aircraft-carrier, *Biter*. On arrival, Walker was to assume overall command of all escorts.

In this one signal, Walker was given an Admiral's responsibility — without an Admiral's staff to share the burden of minute detail. By evening, contact was made and, after placing the two carriers inside the convoy (he was not taking the chance of having another *Audacity* tragedy on his hands), he sent B7 Group fifty miles out on the convoy's starboard bow and placed himself the same distance off the port bow.

With eighteen warships, including the carriers, under his command there was neither rest nor sleep for Walker. Every signal passing between convoy, escort, support groups, Liverpool, London and Newfoundland was repeated to him in case he should think it necessary to intervene. In those rare moments when he could stagger down to his bunk for a brief, restless hour lying fully-dressed in soaked clothes, water seeped in through leaks, forming puddles in the blankets.

On the 25th, the weather subsided to an angry simmer and, now that ON207 was through the danger area, Walker collected *Tracker* and broke off to continue his striking-force hunt. For the next three days, the ships marched and countermarched through the 'Chop' Line in fruitless sweeps backed up by air patrols launched by the carrier, but they found no evidence that there was such a thing as a U-boat in the Atlantic.

At one time, while the weather was hardly suitable for flying but not really bad enough to prevent it, *Tracker* had four aircraft on patrol. They returned in formation and the sloops closed the carrier to act as rescue ships should any of the planes overshoot the flight deck or get into trouble some other way. *Tracker* was rolling heavily and landing would not be easy.

The first aircraft came down, made a beautiful approach and dropped to the deck — but the deck wasn't there. *Tracker* fell into a deep valley of water and the pilot found himself flying when his wheels should have touched down. He overshot the landing wires, hit the deck well for'ard as *Tracker* came up on another wave and then bounced over the side to crash into the sea. Simultaneously, the sloops raced to rescue the aircrew. *Tracker* stopped to try and lower a lifeboat and began drifting rapidly in the wind, bearing down on *Wren* who had reached the wreck first and was lowering a boat herself. For a tense moment it looked as though the rolling edge of *Tracker*'s flight deck would cut off *Wren*'s mast a split second before the carrier ran down both sloop and aircrew. But her engines were racing at full astern and she managed to pull herself clear. Two of the aircrew were picked up; the other was drowned.

More aircraft were still to be brought down. The first of these landed safely more by luck than judgement; the next made a good approach run, but the carrier was tossing heavily and the aircraft was waved round for another attempt. So it went on, with the aircraft making try after try to get down in a succession of moments of suspense until at last it landed, coming to a stop with a broken undercarriage and damaged wings. The men in the sloops wilted with relief. They had been more worried than the pilots. Commander D. S. McGrath, captain of *Tracker*, reported to Walker by R/T: 'Many thanks for your help and moral support. My pilots have resumed their poker in the wardroom and seem to wonder what all the fuss was about.'

On *Starling*'s bridge, Walker chuckled as he turned to Filleul and said admiringly: 'Those chaps have got guts. I wouldn't go near one of those old stringbags on a summer's day, let alone fly them in half a gale in the middle of the Atlantic from a pint-sized flight deck like *Tracker*'s.'

The weather deteriorated again and a full-scale typhoon hit them on November 1st, forcing Walker to order the whole force to heave-to. For three days they headed into the blackness of the storm, only making three knots against mountainous seas which rose like impenetrable green walls above their heads and crashed on the decks with the clash of gigantic cymbals. Overhead, grey watery clouds drove past, propelled by a wind which shrilled with the scream of a thousand violins.

Gun mountings were tom from the decks and thrown aside like so much scrap metal; lifeboats, whalers and motor-boats crumbled into firewood at their davits; galley fires were swamped and men forgot the meaning of feeling dry.

Starling's quarterdeck crack widened and the stern wagged more dangerously; rivets snapped along the ship's side; leaks were sprung in a hundred places. Nothing was immune from the onrush of boiling, tormented seas hungrily searching for victims in every compartment.

The immaculate cruising formation fell apart and ships fought with bows driving against the pounding of waves more to keep in sight of each other than to attempt any form of station-keeping.

Tracker, as the largest ship, became the focal point for the rest. The sloops rose high on boiling crests with joints creaking and propellers threshing wildly in air, before vanishing into deep chasms and gorges of white-streaked, wind-torn water. For seconds, seeming more like eternity, they would be lost from sight only to rise with reluctant groaning. But *Tracker* could be seen by all. She rolled, yawed, tossed and pitched and her flight deck was at times deeper than the bottom of a swimming pool, yet always her radar aerial or control top was visible to red-rimmed eyes peering anxiously from the bridges of the sloops.

After two days of this, Walker called up *Tracker* on the R/T and asked her flight meteorological expert to give an estimate of how long the gales would last. The officer thought they were passing through the edge of the storm and could expect fine weather by the 5th. Unlike the experts who forecast bank holiday weather in peacetime, *Tracker*'s met man was right to the day. The fine weather he predicted came on the morning of the 5th and by noon the sea was reduced to a muttering grumble, allowing Walker to turn the Group towards the 'big game' grounds. Several hours passed before his 'beaters' flushed out the first quarry.

Shortly before midnight the crack of gunfire came from the port end of the line abreast formation and the bleak glare of starshell lit up the water ahead of *Kite*. Immediately, she reported to *Starling* by R/T:

'U-boat on surface two miles ahead of us.'

Walker shouted his orders to the R/T operator:

'*Tracker* alter course to starboard and keep clear of the attack area. *Wild Goose* and *Magpie* to act as carrier screen. *Woodcock* accompany *Starling* to join U-boat hunt with *Kite*.'

The formation dissolved with alarm bells sounding the urgent call to action stations in every ship, with *Wild Goose* and *Magpie* on either bow, *Tracker* turned away from the danger spot. *Woodcock* steamed close on *Starling*'s quarter as she headed at full speed to join *Kite*. The battle was on and Walker, wrapped in a dirty roll-necked pullover and ancient jacket he had worn since taking command of *Starling*, leaned over the front of the bridge looking rather like an eagle about to swoop on some unsuspecting prey.

The enemy, briefly illuminated by the starshell, was a valuable prize — one of Doenitz's few huge 'milch cow' supply U-boats; it had already dived and released SBTs on which *Kite* was unwittingly 'pinging' when Walker arrived. *Starling* made contact and her asdic team shouted out ranges and bearings. In a few minutes, they recognized the decoy echoes and a new search began. By 3 am on the 6th *Starling* found asdic contact with the real target and put the other two sloops on to the U-boat. The night was black and visibility uncertain. Walker decided that with good asdic conditions and an excellent echo, he could afford to wait until daylight before sending *Woodcock* in for the first 'creeping attack'.

After *Woodcock* had been warned to stand by for the first attack after dawn, her captain announced to his ship's company:

'Captain Walker has decided to stay in contact until daylight. Then we shall attack and I expect the U-boat to be destroyed before breakfast.'

For the next four hours, *Starling* jogged along on one engine on a southwesterly course about a mile behind the submerged U-boat. *Kite* and *Woodcock* stayed in close attendance. At 7 am Walker called *Woodcock* alongside and gave her commanding officer instructions over the loudhailer. Crews of three sloops came alert, directors swung on the bearing at which the U-boat might be expected to surface, and depth-charge crews stood by.

Starling stopped with the enemy firmly held in asdic contact while *Woodcock*, asdic silent and engines just turning over to give five knots, crept stealthily along. Just before the ranges and bearings of the enemy coincided, Walker shouted into the R/T: 'Fire now.'

A barrage of twenty-six charges tumbled through the water set to explode at extreme settings of 600 and 800 feet. Said Walker: 'I will stake my last penny on a decisive result to that attack.' None of his officers was inclined to accept the bet. (He would have won. This was *U-220*).

A few minutes later, his asdic operators reported breaking up noises and crunching as though the U-boat was being gripped and squeezed by some colossal hand. Great bubbles of oil spurted to the surface accompanied by wreckage and, an unusual feature, a headless and tailless torpedo. This, with other trophies, was recovered and the three elated sloops altered course to rejoin *Tracker* and her escorts.

As they resumed sweeping stations, Walker hoisted: 'Splice the mainbrace' and *Wild Goose* signalled: *Many congratulations. Magpie and ourselves hope we may play in the first eleven next time.*

Walker had provided *Woodcock* with a trophy and he was not likely to ignore such a plea from *Wild Goose*. Two hours later another U-boat was reported by aircraft to have dived twenty miles away westward of their sweep. Leaving *Kite* and *Woodcock* to take care of *Tracker*, he called out the 'reserve', *Wild Goose* and *Magpie*, and set off at full speed to search the area round the last known diving position.

Once more he showed his gift of being able to anticipate the movements of an opponent. It would take the three sloops more than an hour to reach the diving position and during that time the U-boat could have made good at least five miles in any direction of the compass. By quickly relating the U-boat's position to the convoy routes and taking into account that she might have spotted the aircraft and guessed a carrier force was in the neighbourhood, he swept to northward in the hope of intercepting the enemy. Shortly before 2 pm *Wild Goose* confirmed the accuracy of his mental arithmetic by triumphantly announcing asdic contact. The three ships metaphorically rolled up their sleeves and, while *Magpie* maintained a patrol round the attack area, *Starling* and *Wild Goose* jockeyed into position for the first assault.

Walker attacked with a ten-charge pattern set to 150 and 300 feet to establish the enemy's depth. This run, in his estimation, was so bad it would bear no analysis. 'It was quite shocking,' he wrote later. 'The U-boat took what I thought to be textbook avoiding action — hard over rudder and full speed. In fact, the Boche did nothing of the sort and I missed him by yards.'

Establishing contact again with the enemy at 1,000 yards range, he directed *Wild Goose* into a 'creeping attack' to drop twenty-six charges set to 500 and 700 feet. As the order to fire was given from *Starling*, *Wild Goose* was late in firing her charges and Walker swore with loud violence. The first explosions blew *Starling*'s gyro-compass out of alignment and *Wild Goose* dropped only twenty-two charges. In Walker's view it was a 'thoroughly burn attack and I would have staked my last penny it had failed miserably'.

When the last charge had exploded, he threw his cap to the deck of *Starling*'s bridge and stamped on it in fury. To the amusement of his own crew and that of *Wild Goose* who had steamed close by, he stamped harder and threw his arms up with despair when both ships had reported, *lost contact*. Most of his anger was simulated and designed only to let *Wild Goose* know he was not satisfied with her performance. He was actually sending an acid signal to Wemyss when his own asdic operator calmed him down by reporting breaking up noises and an underwater explosion. In the next few minutes, oil flowed to the surface and spread over a vast area of the sea around them. In the middle of this another headless and tailless torpedo appeared, followed immediately by an abundance of further evidence of destruction.[22]

By the time *Starling*'s whaler had collected the torpedo, a huge block of butter and a glove marked LUICK PIRMANN, Walker admitted he would have lost his last penny. Despite the failure of *Wild Goose* to drop her full pattern of charges, despite *Starling*'s compass being wildly inaccurate, the attack had been effective.

When the three ships left the scene to rejoin *Tracker* and her escorts, the oil had spread for a mile in all directions. It was a jubilant Walker who sent the victory signal to the Group.

At noon on the 8th all the sloops had reached their Prudent Limits of Endurance and Walker ordered the force to set course for Argentia, the United States Atlantic naval base in Newfoundland, where they would refuel and provision for the return voyage.

On the way, one U-boat attacked *Tracker* with two torpedoes from a range of about three miles and HF/DF interceptions showed at least four more in their vicinity, but the Group had insufficient fuel to carry out any hunting. And that night, they ran into the worst gale to strike the Western Atlantic in living memory. For the next two days, the force was hove-to in gigantic, darkly menacing seas. *Starling*'s leaks became larger, her stern wiggling frighteningly as the crack in the quarterdeck widened and spread. While *Tracker* behaved like a double-decker bus on a Big Dipper, the little sloops, battened down but leaking badly, battled night and day against the rushing

---

[22] Confirmed as *U-842*.

rollers. To those whose duties kept them shivering on the bridge or somewhere on deck it seemed that salt water could penetrate the most tightly-wrapped scarf to irritate sore necks and trickle clammily down bare backs. Senses of humour became strained and small things assumed magnified importance. It was not funny when some optimist left open a fan inlet and the fans started to spray sea water instead of air; neither was it amusing when someone else failed to clamp down a skylight and quarts of water cascaded into swinging hammocks.

Meals became regular tests of stamina — for those who could eat. It required an acrobat to sit balanced in a lashed chair and tilt a cup of soup against the bouncing of an unhelpful ship. An extra lurch would send the soup sailing into unprotected and already sodden laps. Once the meal had finished there was the constant internal movement in protesting stomachs — back and forth, up and down. Perhaps the wisest were those who did without. Hammocks bumped against each other and against bulkheads; a rain of condensation showered continually from steel plates of deckheads into the fouled air of closed compartments; exhausted guns' crews and bridge personnel stumbled off watch to lie down and doze restlessly as they were in soaking clothes on tables, lockers and even the hard steel deck itself.

At dawn on the 10th the storm eased enough to allow the Group to proceed at about ten knots; the stinging spray had lost its zest, great seas passed under the ships instead of over them and sudden violent rolls became less frequent. Through the thinning spume and rain squalls the shattered formation began to reappear — all with woeful tales of storm damage. *Woodcock* had suffered worst: one huge wave had smashed into a for'ard gun mounting with its twin guns weighing several tons, ripped it from the desk and cocked the barrels to full elevation; another had crashed against steel ammunition lockers filled with shells and tossed them overboard. It was a battered, weather-scarred and rust-stained line of ships which two days later steamed into Argentia and an unexpected welcome.

On entering the harbour, the Group found themselves being feted by the United States Navy. Hundreds of naval men mixed with sturdy Newfoundlanders to cheer them in. An American dance band from the Officers' Club played their signature tune, 'A-Hunting We Will Go', and as soon as they had tied up dozens of newspapermen and photographers flocked on board.

Walker's name had, in fact, been a byword in the United States Atlantic Fleet for some time, and the highly successful American air and sea units operating against the U-boats west of 'Chop' were impressed with the Second Support Group's record.

Warm as the welcome was, they found greater comfort in the feel of firm, steady ground underfoot; the singing of birds; the smell of burnt rubber on tarmac roads; the blessed release from worry; and sleep, above all sleep, real sleep in steady bunks in strangely quiet ships which no longer rolled, tossed, creaked and groaned.

Walker summed up this terrible voyage briefly: 'What are all these things compared with the satisfaction of having given the Boche more mouthfuls of dust to bite?'

For him, the short respite in Argentia, while the Group carried out stop-gap storm repairs and refuelled, was no rest. He gave a series of lectures to American officers on his methods and then flew to the Royal Navy's convoy terminal at

Halifax, Nova Scotia, to lecture again to Canadian escort officers.

Filleul had an uncle living near Halifax whom he had not seen for many years. When he mentioned this jokingly while Walker was packing a bag for his flight in a plane supplied by the United States Air Force, he was told: 'That's fine, Number One. Get a bag packed and come with me. I'll have a signal sent to Halifax saying you are coming to help me with the lectures.'

John spent the next few days with his uncle, Walker lectured, and the Group as a whole coped with a series of entertainments organized with bewildering generosity by their American hosts. And during this period, Alan Burn was promoted to lieutenant with six months' back seniority, an event which called for a liberal wining with his brother officers.

A week later Walker and Filleul returned to take *Starling* to St John's, the British base in Newfoundland, to stock up with Christmas shopping, the whole crew indulging in a spending spree on food and goods not seen in England since the introduction of rationing. In a Red Cross parcel, Walker found a multi-coloured patchwork leather waistcoat which became his favourite sea rig. Then they sailed to rendezvous with the Group, now minus *Tracker*, bound for the United States, and *Woodcock* which had suffered serious storm damage and had been sent home with a convoy for refit.

Starling, leading *Wild Goose*, *Magpie* and *Kite*, set off across the Atlantic to support hard-pressed convoys routed near the Azores. But it was not until the Admiralty signalled that the east-bound convoy, SL140, had been sighted by Focke-Wulfs and reported to U-boats in the area, that the Group was committed to action again.

The Second and Fourth Support Groups were ordered to the convoy's defence with Walker in overall command. After three days' steaming, the four sloops made contact with the convoy to find the Fourth Group already there. On November 27th the Admiralty signalled that 'pack' attacks could be expected from that night onwards, and leaving the close escort alone, Walker sent the Fourth Group into the deepfield on the starboard bow while his own ships patrolled to port.

By the late evening, HF/DF interception of enemy wireless signalling was reported by all ships in company and they estimated that nine U-boats were shadowing the convoy. *Wild Goose* and *Magpie* were sent to deal with one of the enemy while *Starling* and *Kite* gave chase after another. Subsequent events are described in Walker's Report of the action.

At 2022 (8.22 pm) a searchlight was seen about eight miles away fine on my starboard bow shining upwards and circling, shortly followed by a ripple of firing. I formed the hasty opinion that this could not be a U-boat, but was probably an encounter or alarm by a unit of one or another of the American task forces[23] in the area, with whom I did not want to get mixed up.

The situation was tense and a lively battle imminent. The weather was still rough, the sky overcast and intermittent rain squalls made a pretty dismal background to the threat of heavy enemy attacks. Whatever happened I wanted to keep myself and the Fourth Group free to return at full speed to the defence of the convoy once the balloon went up — although I hoped the Support Groups could break up the packs before they formed up. Conditions were not ideal for this, but it was all we could hope for.

---

[23] Two US striking forces were at sea with the carriers *Rogue* and *Santee*.

I am now thoroughly ashamed of my inaction over the searchlight incident. On cool reflection it was quite obvious that no American task force would come within twenty-five miles of a convoy unheralded. And worse still, it is highly probable that the illumination came from the U-boat we were after, and that it was firing at an aircraft, probably from *Rogue* or *Santee*, I cannot express my regret too deeply. Later, I swept the area for some fifty miles from the convoy with *Kite* in company until we suddenly sighted starshell in the convoy's direction. I turned about and headed back at full speed.

Meanwhile, *Wild Goose* and *Magpie* had sighted a U-boat which dived ahead of them. They attacked but were unable in that weather to gain firm asdic contact. Soon after midnight, *Starling* joined the hunt taking place thirteen miles from the convoy, and an hour later her radar picked up an object ahead. The four sloops fired starshell and illuminated a U-boat on the surface which was at once placed under heavy barrage fire. One hit on the conning-tower blazed redly for a moment and then sizzled out as the enemy crash-dived and vanished underwater. In the next two hours three concentrated 'plaster' attacks were made without result and the Group settled down to match its skill against the U-boat's cunning.

Walker was gazing anxiously over his shoulder at the convoy now under attack and drawing farther away. Snowflake rockets and starshell were being fired in all directions and already the Fourth Group had dropped back into the outfield off the starboard beam to reinforce the defence. The elusive enemy below would have to be sunk quickly or left alone. One more attack failed to bring any evidence of victory to the surface and at 3.30 am Walker ordered the Group to rejoin the convoy at utmost speed.

The battle was over and the brunt had fallen on the Fourth Support Group who had beaten off repeated enemy attacks without the loss of a single ship. They claimed one U-boat probably sunk.

For some reason, the 'pack' failed to attack again and, on December 2nd, Walker's sloops, battered again by the weather and virtually useless for any prolonged action, parted company with the convoy and limped home to Liverpool where they docked on the 5th.

Of this voyage, Walker wrote: 'The new enemy tactics must have been disappointing to them. Clearly they had known about the convoy for many days and had gathered for the usual mass attack. For some unknown reason, however, they failed to follow up the initial attacks. There is no doubt it was intended as a saturation blitz but it proved a complete flop due to the powerful protection supplied by the escort.'

The crews of the Group, however, were not sorry to reach Liverpool with the promise of Christmas at home. They had endured miserable discomfort for weeks in appalling weather. Men and ships needed rest. There was reason to be thankful that neither 'gnats' nor 'Chase-me-Charlies' had appeared to put the final seal on the sheer misery of this voyage. Strain and over-tensed nerves had already taken their toll of *Starling*'s crew. Since commissioning, two officers had been sent ashore unfit for further sea duty, and an able seaman, the best gunner in the ship and a compact sturdy man, had been on leave when he suddenly went berserk with overstrain and was certified insane.

CHAPTER 13: UNDER REPAIR

While still some days out of Liverpool, Walker had sent a signal to Sir Max Horton giving a summary of the damage sustained by the Group and requesting that each ship be placed in dry dock for urgent repairs. Six invaluable dry docks were made immediately available and the Second Support Group was placed on top priority to be repaired, reinforced in design and, in some cases, fitted with the latest equipment.

In his Reports of Proceedings for the whole trip, Walker said:

> In previous reports I have called this class of sloop fine little ships — and so they are in fine weather and in general conception. Bad weather, however, shows up how jerry-built they really are. They leak like sieves and on several occasions I hankered after my sturdy peacetime-built *Stork*.

Referring to operations as a striking force in mid-Atlantic and the sinking of the two U-boats, he wrote:

> I do not know if any of the other Groups have yet used the creeping attack. This is the fourth success in this Group and so far no U-boat has survived to tell the tale — mainly I think because the victim does not know he is being attacked until the charges start exploding all around him.
>
> As regards the value of aircraft-carriers, I think it likely that they will not prove much use in operations with actual convoys unless they can fly off aircraft at night when U-boats are most likely to attack. Their offensive value by day to prevent U-boat concentrations is legendary, but today the only possible time carrier aircraft can hope to sight a U-boat

before she dives is half an hour before dawn and dusk. The chance of seeing a U-boat at periscope depth in the North Atlantic is negligible.

A carrier with a Support Group in winter is nothing but an embarrassment to the Group Senior Officer who is faced with the stipulation that not less than three of his ships must be left to screen her during an attack.

When forwarding this Report to the Admiralty, Admiral Sir Max Horton sent a covering letter saying:

> The destruction of two U-boats on November 6th after no more than a total of seven attacks is a striking example of the ability to achieve kills which is an outstanding attribute of Captain Walker and the Second Support Group. The creeping attack, originated and developed so successfully by Captain Walker, affords little warning to the U-boat — one of the main features of its success. Opportunities to carry out this form of attack are more likely to occur with Support Groups and the attention of commanding officers is once again being drawn to its value.

In Liverpool, the Press had suddenly come alive to the fact that not only was a battle being fought in the Atlantic but that when connected with Captain Walker it was no longer a familiar story of reverses. *Starling* was besieged by reporters and photographers from whom Walker bolted as though the memory of his childhood embarrassment at the Albert Hall was still fresh in his mind. He buried himself at home leaving his officers to cope with the newspapermen.

One morning, Sir Max Horton boarded *Starling* with the Engineer Rear-Admiral on his staff to inspect the damage. Walker, fond of an occasional show of pomp when it could not interfere with the fighting efficiency of his ship or the

Group, welcomed them with a bugler sounding the appropriate calls. Then he escorted the Admirals aft to see a bulkhead which had split open from continual popping backwards and forwards. Next they were taken below and shown the wide crack across the quarterdeck above them. At that moment two stokers on deck turned on firehoses and played jets of sea water on the crack to demonstrate conditions at sea. The water poured through the crack in torrents, nearly drenching the visitors. They left the ship convinced that this class of sloop needed a good deal of strengthening.

For the whole Group, and *Starling* in particular, the weeks in dock passed all too swiftly. During the day, the crews overhauled equipment, learned how to use new instruments, attended courses ashore and in a variety of ways managed to keep themselves busy. In the evenings, there was the occasional dinner for *Starling*'s officers at 'The White House' where Eilleen presided, and more often parties on board *Starling* or some other ship at which Walker stood on his head, drinking a pint of beer. At one party, he challenged Filleul to do it and the eager First Lieutenant, on the excellent assumption that this was one of his captain's achievements which could be equalled, nonchalantly stood on his head and called for the glass of beer. It was intercepted by Captain Walker who solemnly took a firm grip of Number One's trouser leg and poured the beer down it amid a gale of laughter.

Meanwhile, all leave had been stopped in readiness for D-Day and, although Walker argued with the authorities ashore that his men had earned the right to some time with their families, he was allowed to grant local leave only. This meant that they had to live in the same surroundings which for weeks had spelled constant strain and vigilance … an atmosphere which was accentuated rather than relieved by the sudden stop of machinery which normally hums in a ship at sea. At nights a deathly hush fell over *Starling*, and sleep was disturbed and fitful because of it.

During their first days ashore the crew were still wound up from the weeks at sea, still tensed, waiting and humming inside like dynamos. It was hard in those first few days to adjust the inter-locking pattern of life ashore after the small self-contained life of a community at sea. This worried Walker, who disliked punishing men and felt it possible that being confined to Liverpool without the relaxation of home might lead to drunkenness and leave-breaking.

For himself there was little chance to rest. His body could unwind, but his mind was always on his ships and their crews. He talked to Eilleen for hours about his 'chicks', and together they ironed out many domestic problems which were reported to him. As a rule he never intervened in the private lives of his officers or men unless specifically asked to give advice. Even then he was chary of sailing into dangerous, uncharted waters churned up by long separations and hardships.

In the mornings, he visited Derby House to keep abreast of the daily happenings at sea, with a watchful eye on the enemy's tactics and looking for new moves which would call for careful counter-measures when he returned to the battle. The reports from the various fronts of the Atlantic were changing rapidly; a year before they had made sombre reading; now each Intelligence survey provided a tonic and a spur to greater effort.

It is always tempting to look for decisive dates in history, and the greater the field of operations under review the more satisfying the find. In the First World War, March 21st, 1918, stands out as the day on which the Germans began the great offensive which led them by way of victories to utter defeat; a quarter of a century later another decisive date arrived. Up to March 20th, 1943, there had been a real danger that the enemy would achieve his aim of severing the routes which united Great Britain with the North American continent; after that date his strength seemed to ebb and, though the potential power of the U-boat Arm was still enormous, it appeared then that it could be held in check.

The significance of the period up to March 20th, 1943, was that it came close to proving likely that we would not be able to continue convoys as a suitable defence against the enemy's 'pack' tactics. The Admiralty graph of sinkings was again nudging dangerously against the thin red line. After this date, however, the Support Groups, particularly the Second, made an appearance on the battlegrounds and altered the whole strategy of the bitter struggle.

In September, Doenitz made a great effort to retrieve the situation, but his crews were not the men of earlier years. The great autumn offensive failed and the extent of its failure is illustrated by the story of a naval officer ashore in London who was asked by a civilian friend:

'How is the war at sea going?'

Being discreet, the officer gave a non-committal reply.

'There's no need to be quite so discreet,' said his friend. 'I can tell you how it is going. My business is to assemble machines sent over from the United States. At the beginning of the year I was practically at a stop; since the summer, however, I have been working like a man caught in a flood.'

Doenitz was not having much luck with his secret weapons. The 'gnat' was still deadly and a weapon to be reckoned with, but the 'foxer' counter-device was proving fairly effective and U-boat commanders were reluctant to use 'gnats' for their primary purpose of clearing the way through an escort screen to a convoy, preferring to hoard them against the day they would be needed to cripple or sink an attacking escort.

The 'Chase-me-Charlies' were also proving of dubious value. They had been insufficiently tested and were still largely in the experimental stage. They had not yet claimed a totally destroyed victim, though a Canadian escort, HMCS *Athabaskan*, was seriously damaged by one and had to be towed into dock at Devonport. Civilian experts salvaged bits and pieces of the bomb. Their evidence, when coupled with pictures of the bomb taken by sailors who kept their cameras clicking even with the glider-bombs coming straight at them, was sufficient to reconstruct the weapon and discover the sort of fuel which powered the rocket. Bomber Command also carried out a series of nightly attacks on the German plants producing the fuel and, by January 1944, 'Chase-me-Charlies' were making only sporadic, mostly ineffective appearances in the Atlantic battle.

But Doenitz had another trick up his sleeve. It was announced to Western Approaches Command in a general signal from the Admiralty which said:

> U-boats employ a decoy to give a response to radar similar to that given by a U-boat. The device consists of a balloon about two feet six inches in diameter from which is suspended a reflector connected by about fifty feet of thin wire to a wooden float. The reflector consists of a number — about three — of metal-foil strips like pennants one above the other.
>
> U-boats are believed to carry about fifty of these decoys. Once released, the U-boat steams away and the decoy moves down wind at about half the wind speed and remains effective for about four to six hours.

Doenitz had no monopoly of cunning. Two helpful weapons emerged from the Admiralty backroom scientists — a one-ton torpedo-like depth-charge which Walker had called for when he first discovered that U-boats could submerge to more than 800 feet, and a special armour-piercing shell for sinking surfaced U-boats which was called the 'Shark'. The latter, fired from a four-inch gun, hit the water about 100 feet short of a U-boat and continued to travel in a straight line just below the surface to strike the target below the waterline like a tiny torpedo. It would penetrate through the hull and explode inside the U-boat.

The fight for supremacy at sea was beginning to pass from the opposing navies afloat to the scientists ashore.

Soon after the Group was formed in 1943, *Starling* had been 'adopted' by Bootle which boasted that the best of Liverpool docks lay in its boundaries. Now, while the Group was refitting, a ceremony was arranged through Captain (D), Captain Brewer, for the town to be handed the 'General Chase' signals which Walker had used in the Bay of Biscay, and also the Battle Ensigns flown by *Starling* and *Kite* in that and subsequent actions.

During his speech the Mayor, Councillor G. A. Rogers, praised Walker as the Navy's number one U-boat 'killer'. In reply, Captain Brewer said:

'That is quite true. Captain Walker, I think, has not only sex-appeal, but a decided U-boat appeal. At the end of the War, we must give all credit to this officer who in November and December 1941, won the biggest anti-submarine victory of the war while in command of my old ship, *Stork*.'

After handing over the flags in the Town Hall, with Eilleen and most of the *Starling*'s officers present, Walker gave his customary modest reply:

'I do not think I am an "ace" U-boat killer. This kind of warfare is not the sort that has one man as its ace protagonist. Fighting U-boats is very much like playing football or any other sort of game. You have a team of 1,000 men any one of whom can wreck the whole show if he doesn't do his job properly. Every man has his own job to do — I am merely at the head of the affair. So please don't call me U-boat killer number one. That formidable character is 1,000 British tars.'

Nicholas came home for a few days before joining, of all ships, the sloop *Woodcock*. For a moment it looked as though he would sail under his father's leadership, but *Woodcock* was not to return to the Group. Instead she sailed to the Clyde to join the Seventh Escort.

Soon Captain Walker's Group left their various dockyards and re-formed for a short working-up period before setting sail on what was to prove the greatest sea voyage of the Battle of the Atlantic.

CHAPTER 14: THE NELSON TOUCH

Captain Walker took over a Flag Officer's command on January 29th, 1944, when he led his Group from Liverpool to rendezvous off Northern Ireland with the aircraft-carriers, *Nairana* and *Activity*, for a hunting strike into mid-Atlantic. The Group was back to full strength — *Starling*, *Wild Goose*, *Kite*, *Wren*, *Woodpecker* and *Magpie*. After the appalling storms of December, fresh paintwork gleamed dully in a pale wintry sun. Leaks had been plugged, damage repaired, tailwags stopped, and there was every reason for this striking force to be fit, ready and eager to destroy the enemy if he could be found. The carriers' aircraft would be their eyes.

To his officers, Walker confessed his dislike of having to operate with carriers but found some consolation in the hope that they would act as irresistible bait for the U-boats. He grinned appreciatively on the first night out when a bleak half-obscured moon showed both 'flat tops' clearly visible at five miles or more. He mentioned this on the bridge, but the carriers were left in ignorance of their nakedness, it being considered bad for their morale to tell them.

On February 1st they were drawing near to the battleground, steaming in hunting formation, the sloops in line abreast, a mile apart, and the carriers zigzagging independently a mile behind them. Shortly after 10 am all seemed peaceful enough; it was a crisp, cold morning with a slight swell and calm sea. In *Starling*, Alan Burn had exercised his guns' crews, *Woodpecker* had carried out depth-charge drill, and in *Wild Goose* on the port extreme of the line, Commander Wemyss was discussing their 'dead reckoning' position with his navigator in the chartroom. Suddenly a shout came down the bridge voicepipe.

'Captain, Sir, submarine echo to starboard.'

Wemyss rushed to the bridge, and a quick report from the asdic operator made it clear that it was a U-boat trying to penetrate the screen for a close shot at the bait. Wemyss turned to look back at the carrier and, to his horror, saw *Nairana* turn on a zig to port bringing her in the enemy's direction. At any moment she would be sitting squarely in the U-boat's sights. Wemyss rapped out orders.

'Hard a'starboard.... Full speed.... Hoist attacking flag.... Tell Leader on R/T I am attacking.'

The enemy had passed between *Wild Goose* and her neighbour, *Magpie*, by the time Wemyss had turned his ship and was slithering in for the first attack. Wemyss blinked a warning to *Nairana* to get out of the way and without waiting for a perfect run-in, dropped a ten-charge pattern more to scare the enemy than to sink him. *Nairana* was still in danger.

As soon as he received Wemyss's report, Walker flashed a signal to *Nairana* ordering her to head out to starboard at full speed. He repeated the order to *Activity* and told off *Kite*, *Wren* and *Woodpecker* to screen them. Then he headed towards the battle while *Wild Goose* was drawing off and *Magpie* about to follow with another attack. This yielded no result and *Magpie* was sent off to assist in screening the carrier, leaving *Wild Goose* and *Starling* to continue the hunt.

'Unquestionably, *Nairana* was saved by *Wild Goose*'s exemplary speed and decision,' Walker said later. 'Another minute or two and she would have been a sitter. When *Magpie* had left to join the remainder of our force, *Wild Goose* handed me asdic contact with the Boche on a plate. I could ask nothing better than to take the field again partnered by this doughty, well-trained warrior. Conditions were good, though the wind was rising and stirring up the sea a bit.'

Walker followed quietly behind the U-boat for a while, calculating that she was steaming at about four knots very deep. He decided to carry out a two-ship 'Operation Plaster'. Line abreast and close, *Starling* and *Wild Goose* went in to the attack at five knots, dropping in all some sixty-odd depth-charges set to explode between 500 feet and 700 feet at five-second intervals. In their wake the depth-charges detonated in a continuous crackling roar like an express train tearing through a tunnel. The sea split and heaved under the explosions and even the experienced sailors, accustomed as they were to the weight and ferocity of Walker's methods, were stunned by the nonstop crashing and cracking from below the surface.

Walker was in effect using his depth-charges as main armament and firing them in salvoes as though from guns. *Starling*'s crew were startled when, while all were gazing astern at the exploding sea, a bang shook them from ahead and a gush of water appeared over the bows. This could hardly be a depth-charge. After a few minutes Walker ordered 'Cease Fire' and both ships stood by to wait for tangible evidence of a sinking.

It was not long in coming. Oil, clothing, planks of wood, pulped lifejackets, books and the mangled remains of bodies provided all the evidence needed of death and destruction far below them. Using the loudhailer, Walker shouted to Wemyss to follow him and, as the two ships rejoined the carriers, *Starling* flew from her yardarm the eagerly expected signal: 'Splice the mainbrace'. In this way, the 740-ton underwater raider *U-502* was destroyed.

Five uneventful days later, the sloops refuelled from *Activity* and received orders to support the west-bound convoy SL147 which was believed to be heading for trouble. Quick calculations in *Starling* showed to everyone's joy that a large 'pack' was gathering and the Group could arrive in time for the impending battle.

The striking force made contact with SL147 on February 7th and Walker took overall command of the escort. Leaving the close escort group in their stations, he placed his sloops round the convoy as an outer screen six miles out. *Nairana* and *Activity* were ordered to operate their aircraft in the deepfield by day and to enter into the middle of the convoy at night.

During the 7th, Admiralty reports of U-boats heard chattering by wireless in the convoy's vicinity indicated a 'pack' of about ten. Next day, the pack increased until it became likely that at least fifteen U-boats were converging for the fatal pounce. Tension grew as warning signals poured in during the afternoon. After an exchange with the Commodore, Walker sent a general message ordering all ships to action stations at nightfall.

He stayed happily on his bridge all that day, well wrapped-up in his fading old grey pullover and stained leather waistcoat. With one U-boat already destroyed on this voyage, the 1944 season had opened well for his Group. He would have been just as cheerful had he known that no fewer than twenty-six U-boats were in contact and waiting for the cover of darkness to spring upon their prey — a convoy of eighty-one ships with two aircraft carriers looming high in the centre.

As dusk faded into darkness, the night became eerie; a heavy damp mist settled over the scene, covering ships and men in a white frost-like dew; sea and sky merged in a haze of deep midnight blue gradually blotting out the horizon until the ships seemed to be flying through thin, wispy, low-lying cloud. A hush settled over both sea and ships and the darkness closed in, muffling all sounds other than the swish of bows cutting into green, unfriendly water.

To Walker and the thirteen other warship commanders it was a game of patience, waiting to see from which quarter the enemy would make his first lunge. To the eighty-one Merchant Navy captains it was more like roulette. Whose number would come up first? Which of them would be the first to explode in flames?

Wild Goose was six miles ahead of the convoy on the port quarter and it fell to her port bridge lookout, Able Seaman J. G. Wall, a young reservist sailor, to sound the alarm which rang through the silence to be repeated in dozens of ships spread across miles of the Atlantic. Raking his sector with binoculars on this deathly black night, he beat the radar by sighting a U-boat trimmed down on the surface with only her conning-tower showing at a range of nearly a mile and a half.

His report, shouted excitedly to a tense group of officers on the bridge, sparked off the warning and, as the close escort hugged their charges protectively, Walker ordered the convoy to make a drastic alteration of course. The enemy had launched their attack; now his sloops could get down to the earnest business of killing.

Wild Goose turned towards the U-boat, increased to full speed and prepared to ram. The enemy, realizing he had been sighted, crash-dived. When the sloop arrived only a swirl of water marked the spot. But the enemy captain was curious and, instead of diving deep and taking avoiding action, he stayed at periscope depth to keep track of *Wild Goose*'s movements in the hope of slipping past her and continuing his swoop on the convoy.

Again it was Able Seaman Wall who succeeded where instruments failed. A shout brought Commander Wemyss to the side of his bridge to gape in astonishment, while Wall pointed to a periscope poking out of the water approximately twenty yards away. Wemyss fumed; he was searching the area with his asdic and going too slow to punish the enemy's impertinence with a shallow-set pattern of depth-charges. His machine gunners had just enough time to pepper the two or three feet of periscope with fire — scoring several hits — before the U-boat commander, anticipating the awful retribution which might follow his impudence, downed periscope and dived away.

Wild Goose obtained asdic contact in time to direct the newly-arrived *Woodpecker* into a creeping attack. When the last depth-charge had exploded, Walker raced up, took one look at the surging water and signalled *Woodpecker*: 'Look what a mess you have made.' After some crackling cross-chat, the three sloops regained contact with the enemy and settled down to the attack formula — convoy, aircraft-carriers, close escort and the rest of the Group steaming rapidly out of danger.

Walker directed *Woodpecker* into the first attack while *Wild Goose* prepared to follow. Firing her charges, *Woodpecker* slowly moved over the U-boat, dropping twenty-six set to explode at maximum depth. A few moments of expectant silence fell after the last charge had detonated; then a tremendous explosion came from the depths below and for a fraction of a second the sea was petrified into immobility, before boiling in angry confusion. Another of Doenitz's prized fleet, *U-762*, was destroyed, blown apart by the depth-charging and finally disintegrating under the impact of an internal explosion.

The three sloops fired snowflake rockets to illuminate the scene and, in their bleak flare, pieces of wreckage could be seen floating forlornly on waves blackened and quietened by the weight and flow of the U-boat's oil. *Starling* lowered a boat, and collected a German coat and other evidence of destruction before Walker led the three triumphant ships back to the convoy. It was shortly after midnight and the score was one up and more to come.

Kapitanleutnant Hartwig Looks, a U-boat officer since 1936 and now captain of *U-264* with 14,000 tons of Allied shipping to his credit, had lost the convoy. He had been in contact since the previous morning, knew there were probably twenty of his brother U-boats in the vicinity with more arriving at regular intervals and decided to launch his attack on SL147 at midnight on the night of February 8th/9th. It was a large convoy and he had hopes of more than usual success. His ship was the first in the U-boat Arm to be fitted with that ingenious extensible diesel air intake and exhaust device which allowed U-boats to 'breathe'. Instead of having to surface to charge its batteries, *U-264* could stay submerged at periscope depth with the 'Schnorkel' poking up like a periscope. This meant he could submit to a prolonged destroyer hunt without having to surface.

Shortly before midnight, an escort force had come chasing towards him and he had dived thinking they were about to attack. The exploding depth-charges had fallen quite near, but. far enough away for Looks to be tolerably certain someone else and not *U-264* was under attack. Looks took his boat deep and continued on the same course as the convoy had been steering all day. At a crucial moment his hydrophones broke down and he could no longer hear the convoy's propellers. Taking a gamble, he stayed on course and came up to periscope depth to check his position in relation to the convoy.

His quarry had altered course and Looks saw nothing but darkness as he turned the periscope in a complete circle. Inwardly furious, he brought *U-264* to the surface and headed northwards in the hope of finding other prey.

Soon after *Starling*, *Wild Goose* and *Woodpecker* had resumed their stations, the close escorts to port of the convoy beat back a skirmish with two U-boats creeping in on the surface. The action was too far away and over too quickly for Walker to play any part in the proceedings.

The night was enlivened further by the sudden roar of aircraft engines followed by the brilliant glare of flares dropped over the convoy in an attempt to provide the U-boats with silhouetted targets. It seemed, however, that the 'pack' were not to be tempted even by their flying brethren. No attack followed and, somewhat mystified, Walker had to wait until just before 6 am when all ships of the Group and the close escort intercepted by HF/DF a U-boat signalling by wireless on the surface.

Bearings put the enemy ten miles ahead of the convoy, so he ordered *Magpie* and *Kite*, the nearest sloops, to investigate. Fifteen minutes later, while *Magpie* was still some distance astern of *Kite* and racing to catch up, the U-boat was suddenly sighted as it came out of a patch of mist steaming fast towards the convoy and only 800 yards away from *Kite*. Her commanding officer's instinctive reaction to Walker's long and patient training was to realize instantly the danger of being attacked by 'gnats'. As the U-boat crash-dived, he reduced speed to seven knots and fired a single depth-charge in the hope of counter-mining a 'gnat' torpedo before it could strike home. A second or two later a violent explosion threw up a column of water twenty yards on *Kite*'s port beam.

Her captain's fears had been well founded. The U-boat had fired while diving and the depth-charge explosion had set off the 'gnat' warhead causing a double explosion. Immediately, *Kite* increased to full speed and ran over the diving position to fire a full pattern of ten depth-charges. This brought no result and, after *Magpie* joined, the two ships gained asdic contact and settled down to a classic Walker hunt.

At the moment *Kite* and the U-boat sighted each other, *Wild Goose* obtained radar contact with another U-boat little more than a mile away on the convoy's port bow. Also fearing a 'gnat' torpedo, she reduced speed to seven knots and fired off starshell. The first salvoes revealed the U-boat about to dive, and a few seconds later a loud explosion was heard astern. A 'gnat', having failed to pick up her slow-revving propellers, had missed and exploded at the end of its run.

Wild Goose's first depth-charge attack at shallow settings drove the U-boat deep and, by the time Walker came up in *Starling*, he was again handed asdic contact 'on a plate'. By 8.30 am Walker had directed *Wild Goose* on two creeping attacks and carried out another himself during which another 'gnat', unable to home itself on to targets moving at slow speeds, detonated at the end of its run, a few hundred yards astern of *Starling*.

Although the crews of the three sloops were well aware that slow speeds were the best defence against this deadly weapon, the men could not help showing some anxiety. It was not natural to amble slowly about the ocean while the enemy fired torpedoes; especially worried were the depth-charge crews on the quarterdecks who would be the first to suffer should a 'gnat' prove hypersensitive and 'hear' even the slowest revolutions.

Half an hour later oil came to the surface — but the U-boat was still on its feet, if a little groggy.

At 9 am the convoy, carriers and close escort steamed between the two battle grounds, each about six miles on either side of it. As they cleared the area, the senior officer of the close escort signalled Walker: *Good luck, hope to see you again.* The reply came: *We seem to have nabbed a couple of particularly tough babies. Will be rejoining soon.*

This was nearly wishful thinking. *Starling* was only just moving when suddenly a chorus of amazed, urgent shouts came from all parts of the ship. Walker spun round and, only a few hundred yards away, the shallow-running torpedo could be seen streaking towards them. There was no time to pick up speed and take avoiding action. The enemy had come up to periscope depth, fired an ordinary torpedo at a sitting target and gone down again. Walker's mind raced: unless he found a way out in the next few seconds, *Starling* would be a blazing, sinking wreck. With eyes fixed on the bubbling track of the deadly missile, he gave orders.

'Hard a'port.... Stand by depth-charges.... Shallow setting.... Fire.'

The crew, many of whom had already run to the far side away from the expected explosion while others had thrown themselves flat on the deck, were astounded to hear a command for the charges to fire at shallow setting while their ship was dawdling along. The explosions would blow the stern off.

Suddenly the air was torn by two almost simultaneous, shattering roars. The first came from the depth-charges, and the second, by far the more frightening, from the torpedo which had gone off only five yards from *Starling*'s quarterdeck. A lightning decision, coupled with instant and disciplined obedience, had certainly saved the ship and countless lives —

for the depth-charges had counter-mined the torpedo a second before it struck home against *Starling*'s thinly-plated hull.

A huge wave pyramided vertically high above *Starling*'s masthead, the sloop shook and jerked as though being shaken by some gigantic hand; reserve depth-charges were thrown overboard by the shock blast, luckily failing to explode; tons of water fell in solid green sheets over the depth-charge crew standing momentarily stunned on the quarterdeck but still doing their duty automatically; all electrical switches were thrown open in the power rooms; and worse, every bottle in the wardroom was shattered into fragments.

Starling gathered speed and shook herself clear of the swilling water while depth-charges continued to leave the ship in the strict, methodical pattern of the creeping attack. There was not a hitch or delay in the drill. Remarkably, *Starling* had suffered no damage and on the bridge Walker murmured, 'Interesting. This chap seems to know his job. It's almost a pity to think we shall kill him without ever seeing what he's like.'

In the next half hour, Walker directed *Wild Goose* on two more creeping attacks and followed up with both ships carrying out an 'Operation Plaster'. In this last run, he took his revenge and delivered the death blow. A few minutes later a loud underwater explosion cracked to the surface and soon a huge air bubble boiled up and collapsed spreading chunks of wood and human remains over hundreds of feet of sea. At 10 am, after collecting wreckage and other evidence, *Starling* and *Wild Goose* steamed off to assist *Kite* and *Magpie*. *U-734* had gone the way of so many others, but it had taken nearly 150 depth-charges dropped over more than three hours to destroy her. And she had come closer than any U-boat to destroying *Starling*.

On joining *Kite* and *Magpie* at noon Walker found that they had carried out a series of creeping attacks without result. As *Kite* had first made contact with the U-boat, he sent *Wild Goose* and *Magpie* to patrol the area, gained contact himself and directed *Kite* into two more attacks, using more than fifty depth-charges.

In this last attack, the enemy showed himself as cunning and tough as the one before. As *Kite* steamed in slowly to begin her depth-charge barrage, a 'gnat' was fired in self-defence. While it was still twenty yards away, the first depth-charges set off immediately counter-mined the torpedo — which *Kite* had not yet seen. There was a thunderous crash and, to *Starling*'s crew, it looked as if their sister ship had been hit squarely amidships. For long heart-stopping seconds, the wide column of thin green water hovered over the shocked, surprised *Kite*. Cheers rang out from *Starling*'s men, as first *Kite*'s mast appeared, then her bridge, and finally the whole ship — unbelievably, wonderfully intact. She had shuddered and kicked under the impact of the blast, but was still on course and the depth-charges were tumbling from her racks and shooting from her throwers in well-drilled precision. There had been no faltering in the continuity of the attack.

But the sloop was badly shaken and several leaks had been sprung in her stern. She had only seventeen depth-charges left, so Walker sent her out to the touchline and brought *Magpie* in for the next assault. With *Starling* acting as directing ship, *Magpie* now carried out a twenty-six-charge creeping attack with the same result — nothing.

On *Starling*'s bridge, Walker grinned appreciatively. This was an opponent worthy of his best. Twisting, altering his depth constantly, the enemy commander was making every attack fall wide of the mark. Walker worked out a new procedure on the spot. *Magpie* was equipped with 'Hedgehog', the multi-barrelled mortar bomb thrower which could destroy only if one or more bombs scored direct hits. He would direct her in for a 'Hedgehog' barrage and follow up with a depth-charge attack himself. When he announced this to *Starling*'s officers — there were chuckles all round. Imagine aiming another ship's weapons to fire twenty-four bombs and expect any of them to score direct hits on a target 70 feet below.

'I was highly tickled by this hedgehoggery,' he wrote later. 'Complicated instruments are normally deemed essential to score an occasional hit with this weapon. But under my orders over the R/T, *Magpie* steamed in to attack and fired off her bombs when told as if firing depth-charges for a creeping attack. The result was an immediate double explosion which shook both ships. To score two bullseyes like that first shot with somebody else's Hedgehog 1,000 yards away was, of course, a ghastly fluke, but amusing considering no instruments at all were used.'

This unorthodox and unscientific attack had without doubt succeeded. To make sure, Walker accepted the risk that the enemy might still be capable of firing 'gnats'. At 3.30 pm *Starling* raced in at full speed for a ten-charge pattern set deep. A few seconds later, when the crashing roar of the last depth-charge had died away, the remains of *U-238* bobbed sadly on the surface. *Magpie* was now a fully-blooded member of the Group.

Walker had been in command of the battle for nearly thirty-six hours without break. With eighty-one merchant ships depending on him, two aircraft-carriers hoping he would protect them, a close escort screen of six warships feeling unhappily impotent in their role of static defenders, and his own sloops spoiling for trouble in the outfield, he had faced one of the most dangerous 'pack' attacks of the war and ripped it apart by killing three of the enemy in relentless thrusts and beating off less skilled raiders. This had been done without loss in ships, and at least 140 Germans had died while the British sailors had not suffered even a slight wound.

Tired, but seemingly fresh; outwardly matter-of-fact yet inwardly tensed and fizzing with excitement at the victory, Walker was outspoken in his criticism of certain parts of his Group's efforts during the night; but in his heart deeply proud and content with every one of them.

The Group stayed with SL147 until the following morning, the 10th, but the crippled enemy failed to appear. At dawn, after exchanging signals with the Commodore, the aircraft-carriers and the close escort, *Starling*, *Wild Goose*, *Woodpecker*, *Kite*, *Wren* and *Magpie* formed up in line abreast, hunting formation, and set course for another convoy, HX277, which included the Norwegian tanker, *Thorsholm*, fully stocked with depth-charges to replenish escorts in the unfortunate position of *Starling* and *Kite*.

Re-ammunitioning with depth-charges at sea was a long, tedious and nerve-racking business requiring skill, patience and an even temper. Walker snatched his first two hours of sleep for nearly three days while the Group was en route, but the afternoon of the 10th spent steering alongside the *Thorsholm* proved the most gruelling experience of the voyage. Only twenty-five yards apart and rolling heavily in a high swell the two ships steamed together, each of the tanker's rolls threatening to capsize the sloop. The depth-charges were hauled over by hand singly, at times sinking below the surface or being carried away to bump dangerously against the ship's side as both sending and receiving ships rose and fell unevenly on the swell.

To avoid the whole Group being immobilized, Walker ordered *Wren* to stand by while *Wild Goose*, *Woodpecker* and *Magpie* sailed off to support a following convoy, HX278. The Group was all keyed to carry the battle to the enemy; any let-down now would accentuate their weariness and Walker was keen on getting *Starling* back into commission with the power to punch hard. At dusk, he called a halt to the ammunitioning and headed south at full speed with *Kite* and *Wren* to join the rest sweeping far astern of the convoy.

So many signals of congratulation had been received from Liverpool and the Admiralty — each was read out to the crews of all ships by their commanding officers — that there was an air of carefree omnipotence around. The knowing ones on the mess decks were no longer taking bets on whether the Group would make a 'kill' this trip, but on how many and at what time the next would be sighted.

Wild Goose, *Woodpecker* and *Magpie* swept astern the track of convoy HX278 in the hope of pouncing on stragglers or shadowers who might be still on the surface. Success came quickly; during the middle or 'graveyard' watch between midnight and 4 am on the 12th, the three ships stumbled over a submerged marauder creeping up on the convoy from the stern. *Wild Goose*, usually first of the Group to join battle, made contact, and Commander Wemyss, still suffering from a won't-be-stared-at-through-periscopes complex from his last struggle, went into attack. But *Magpie* had somehow manoeuvred into the way and *Wild Goose* had to swerve hurriedly in the middle of her run to avoid collision.

Wemyss resumed the attack with the range so close that he was still going slow when his depth-charges exploded, nearly lifting the sloop out of the water with the blast force. Asdic conditions were not good — in certain sea areas the beams became distorted — and the three ships had an uncomfortable time gaining, losing and regaining contact with a slippery opponent who snaked freely about the ocean at varying depths.

After an hour of attack during which some fifty-odd depth-charges were dropped, *Wild Goose* made firm contact at last and Wemyss, tired of what he called 'this groping around and dot and carry one business' went in for a full-blooded 'plaster' attack. After the sea had died down, the tensed, anxious sloops were rewarded with a heavy roar of underwater crunching and breaking-up noises.

For a few minutes the noises continued, then oil and wreckage came rushing to the surface. The trio reported by R/T to Walker who was hurrying to the scene with *Kite* and *Wren*, and resumed their patrol.

He arrived next morning and steamed through the area inspecting the bits and pieces floating in the oil, but he refused to credit the Group with another 'kill' because an aircraft had claimed a sinking in almost the same position and *Starling*'s doctor was unable to declare samples of the pulped flesh as human. U-boats had been known to take slaughtered animals to sea and fire them to the surface, when under attack, in the hope of fooling the hunters.

At noon the two sections of the Group united and Wemyss insisted he had destroyed the U-boat in his last attack. Walker therefore decreed they should all patrol back to the scene to investigate the wreckage more carefully. They returned at 5 pm and, by this time, the oil patch spread over an area six miles in diameter, and convincing human and other remains were awaiting collection.

'I might well have realized,' said Walker later, 'that an officer of *Wild Goose*'s experience knows what he is talking about when he reports breaking-up noises, etc. It was an undoubted kill.' So ended the career of the 740-ton *U-424*.

While Commander Wemyss and his officers were celebrating their victory the idea of giving *Wild Goose* a ship's banner was born. When he had commanded a submarine during the First World War, Sir Max Horton had flown a black flag on returning to harbour to signify a successful voyage. This flag carried the skull and cross-bones and bore other strange devices to commemorate the submarine's exploits.

Wemyss could see no reason why an anti-submarine vessel such as *Wild Goose* should not do the same, although in discussion with his officers he insisted that the design should be dignified as befitted the sloop's size and appearance.

'The outcome,' he says, 'was a really handsome banner. It was dark blue in colour with the ship's crest in white in the middle.' As the Second Support Group celebrated 'kills' by splicing the mainbrace, it was decided to portray the victories by drawing empty grog casks in the top right-hand corner. The design having been approved by their captain, the crew of *Wild Goose* settled down to have the banner ready for entering harbour.

After this patrol, the Group sailed to the support of a westward-bound convoy, ON224, from which Walker decided to take on more depth-charges. He took twenty-six from the Panamanian tanker *Belgian Gulf* who also sent across a waterproof bag containing bottles of brandy and cigarettes.

That night Walker took overall command of the three forces — the close escort, the Seventh Support Group and his own Group — in readiness for a fight through an area reportedly jammed with U-boats. The next two days saw only minor skirmishes and, on the 19th, he led the Group away to retrace the convoy's course in another attempt to catch unawares any of the enemy who might be shadowing. He reported this decision to Liverpool and received in reply a signal telling him to stay with the convoy.

By that time the Group were in line abreast some nineteen miles astern of the convoy and, like Nelson before him, Walker turned a blind eye, intending to disobey only for a few minutes while they investigated a weak contact reported by *Woodpecker*. This turned out to be a firm U-boat contact. Ignoring the signal entirely, Walker formed up his ships for the hunt.

For the last ten days since leaving convoy SL147, *U-264* had been wandering around the mid-Atlantic battlefield seeing a lot of activity without actually taking part. Captain Looks was still confident of his 'Schnorkel' breathing device which had enabled him to stay submerged and out of trouble at times when he would have been forced to surface in most embarrassing circumstances.

With some confidence he attacked ON224 during the night of February 18th/19th. He was somewhat less confident when he succeeded only in bringing a destroyer of the close escort screen racing across to bombard him with depth-charges for the next two hours. Eventually the destroyer gave up the hunt and *U-264*, with a chastened and grumbling crew, slunk away to the stern of the convoy. Shortly after 10 am the menacing bows of the Second Support Group filled Looks' periscope and he gave the order to dive deep.

Throughout the 19th, in heavy seas, with a gloomy overcast sky and a high wind, the Group attacked their target, but asdic conditions were poor and they kept losing contact. One creeping attack after another was producing no more result than to disturb the already highly angry seas and by 4 pm the battle had settled down to one of endurance. But if Walker and his Group felt capable of continuing the struggle until a decisive result was achieved, Looks knew that time was running out.

The continuous depth-charging had caused havoc inside *U-264*. Her lights had failed, her engines had been shaken loose from their mountings, the new 'Schnorkel' had broken down and one propeller shaft had jammed. The attack went on and the noise of the crashing, roaring, exploding depth-charges made it impossible to hear anything on the hydrophones. Looks decided that he would have to surface and abandon ship.

At 5 pm exactly he broke surface a mile from the Second Support Group whose guns bore down and blazed into action. On the bridge of *Starling*, a wild-looking figure in a patchwork waistcoat stood on the chart table, waving his hat in the air and cheering as each shell exploded in a dull red flash against the U-boat.

On the conning-tower, despite his desperate plight, the captain of *U-264* gave the order, 'Abandon Ship', and stood by until the last of his crew had leapt into the water. Then he went below, set the scuttling charges and, with shells hitting the U-boat at every salvo, saluted and dived overboard. Seven minutes later, *U-264* sank stern first. The complete crew of seven officers, nine petty officers and thirty-five ratings were rescued and taken aboard *Starling*, *Wild Goose* and *Woodpecker*,

Walker signalled the Group to splice the mainbrace. In his report he wrote: 'The enemy threw in the towel after receiving a big wallop in the belly from *Starling*'s last creeping attack.'

The Group had just re-formed when *Kite* reported engine defects and had to be detached to return to Liverpool. She was never to rejoin the Group. After completing her repairs, she reinforced another striking force covering Russian convoys in icy, Arctic waters. There she was torpedoed and sunk, all but seven of her ship's company of more than 150 men going down with her. In those icy seas, it was impossible for a man to live longer than minutes.

Kite's departure left an empty feeling in the Group who knew that with damaged engines she would have to pass through dangerous areas at slow speeds. That night, shortly before midnight, while the sloops were steaming in line abreast, a heavy explosion sounded from somewhere on *Starling*'s port beam. Walker, who had been snatching a few moments' rest in his sea cabin, rushed to the bridge and the Officer of the Watch pointed out two flares sparking on the surface about four miles away. They were startled again by three more explosions, swiftly followed by an urgent call on the R/T.

It was *Woodpecker* reporting her stern blown off by a 'gnat' torpedo. The first explosion had been the 'gnat' hitting her, the flares being automatically set off from her spare life jackets when they hit the water, and the last three explosions had been depth-charges going off from her sinking stern. In seconds every man in the Group knew what had happened and was shocked at the disaster; for too long they had believed themselves indestructible.

Without thinking of revenge, the Group formed a protective screen round their stricken sister ship and, after half an hour, *Woodpecker* was able to report no one hurt and that she was capable of staying afloat. Relief flowed through the ships; they were still invincible and the enemy could not claim a victim yet. Walker, indifferent shiphandler but brilliant seaman, decided to do the towing himself while the Group acted as an escort. While closing in to pass over a towing line, he nearly finished off the U-boat's job by colliding with *Woodpecker*. But he grazed her side and eventually the operation was successfully completed and *Starling*, with *Woodpecker* in tow, was making about four knots in the general direction of the United Kingdom.

However, the weather was too rough and, after the tow lines had parted several times, Walker signalled Liverpool asking for tugs to be sent to their assistance. On the 21st the oceangoing tug, *Storm King*, arrived and took the tailless *Woodpecker* in tow at a cracking rate of six knots and on an accurate course for Liverpool. All except a skeleton crew were transferred to the other sloops. Handing over their damaged 'chick' to another escort Group, the sloops headed for home.

The Group was on its last legs; ammunition was low, depth-charges had been expended and fuel exhausted in non-stop attack and counter-attack. Officers and men were haggard, irritable and jumpy under the constant strains of alarms and the fear of 'gnats'.

While they steamed, red-eyed and drawn, towards base, the grey Atlantic took a hand in the towing of *Woodpecker*. Great rolling seas piled up around the helpless ship and gallant little tug; huge, mocking breakers crashed heavily on the sloop until her captain ordered the skeleton crew to abandon ship. The last man had jumped into a tiny lifeboat and pulled clear when *Woodpecker* heaved into the air, twisted and writhed as though in mortal agony, then leaned over on her side, finally to capsize and sink with a long, low groan of escaping air. Only rapid action by the tug, *Storm King*, saved her from being dragged under with her charge. The first of the Second Support Group had been destroyed, not by the enemy, but by the impartial, vindictive sea.

Almost at the same time, Walker, leading the Group up the Irish Sea, received a signal from the Admiralty saying that the

Prime Minister and the War Cabinet wished to convey their congratulations on the excellent work performed by the Second Support Group.

Worn out but happy, they sailed in line ahead towards Liverpool; now the shorter, choppy seas of coastal waters replaced the long Atlantic rollers and heralded sanctuary and sleep. With the need for action stations and alarms gone, the spirited internal rivalry between the Group supplied an outlet for over-tensed nerves.

While Walker paced the bridge of *Starling*, leaving his Officer of the Watch to handle the ship, signal lamps blinked domestically ribald messages which he considered it wise to ignore.

To *OOW Wild Goose* from *OOW Starling* — *You are astern of station.*

To *OOW Starling* from *OOW Wild Goose* — *Why don't you keep a steady speed. You are travelling in leaps and bounds like a kangaroo.*

To Navigator *Starling* from Navigator *Wild Goose* — *You are leading us slap into the middle of a minefield.* This was a direct attack on *Starling*'s leadership and her navigator indignantly rushed into his chartroom to make a rapid check on his course. A few minutes later he reappeared on the bridge with seeming unconcern to tell the Yeoman of Signals:

'Make an appropriate reply, Yeoman. Not more than one word.'

The Group were still some hours out of Liverpool when *Starling*'s doctor was transferred to *Wren* to assist her medical officer in an urgent operation for acute appendicitis which proved successful. As Burn remarked irreverently afterwards: 'Both those Docs would try anything once.'

In this mood the sloops arrived off Liverpool to be met by the training ship, *Philante*, carrying the flag of Admiral Sir Max

Horton, a fast piece of regulation signalling informing them that also aboard was the First Lord of the Admiralty, Mr A. V. Alexander.

Philante steamed down the line of ships signalling to each the First Lord's congratulations on the successes of their voyage. As they passed, he could be seen through a porthole wearing a dressing-gown and hurrying to get dressed in time to wave in person from *Philante*'s bridge.

The Group entered the swept channel in line ahead 200 yards apart and steamed into harbour majestically, maintaining station as rigidly as a line of guardsmen with guns laying fore and aft, White Ensigns flying stiffly in the breeze. From *Wild Goose*'s masthead fluttered the victory banner with the strange devices.

As the line of sturdy 'little ships' approached Gladstone Dock, nearly 2,000 officers, sailors, Wrens, civilian port employees and dockyard workers lining both sides of the docks cheered and waved wildly, while at Captain (D)'s signal station a proud signal ran up:

Johnnie Walker still going strong.

Two military bands combined to play *Starling*'s signature tune 'A-Hunting We Will Go'. Tied up opposite the Group's berths, an aircraft-carrier and an American destroyer flew signals of congratulations and their crews manned the sides to join in the cheering.

Philante went past first and from *Starling*'s bridge they could see the First Lord, the Commander-in-Chief and several Staff officers take their places ashore for the official welcome.

It took a few moments for Walker to understand what all the fuss was about. Soon he had entered into the spirit of the occasion and ordered his First Lieutenant to see that the ships and the crews were smartened up as soon as possible.

Inwardly, he was as excited as a schoolboy at Christmas time; outwardly, the only indication of his pride in his ships was the usual broad grin which sparkled into a smile of joy when he saw Eilleen, Nicholas home on leave, and Gillian standing near Mr Alexander and Sir Max.

Captain (D) had sent a car for the family earlier in the morning — a dull grey, typically Liverpool morning — and when they arrived, Mr, now Sir, Reginald Hodges, of the Mersey Docks and Harbour Board, greeted Eilleen and took her across to the group from *Philante*.

A Staff officer was the first aboard to warn Filleul that crews were to be paraded ashore to be inspected and addressed by the First Lord. A low moan passed from the wardroom to the mess decks as the news spread. Although some first-aid work on the sloops had followed the captain's order, they were hardly in a state to be inspected; bearing the scars of a 7,000-mile cruise in which they had been in almost continuous contact with the enemy. Officers and men were desperately tired and wanted nothing more than to be allowed to sleep undisturbed.

For a while, minor panic reigned. Someone found a battered bugle; and a sailor who could barely remember the last time he had seen the instrument was locked away in a remote part of the ship to polish up both the bugle and his version of the various calls required to impress the First Lord and Commander-in-Chief.

Walker's first thought was for his family. Before the gangway had been put across, he helped Eilleen to step over to the ship's rail and on to the deck and led her to the wardroom, where with other officers' wives she waited while the formalities were dealt with first. A battalion of newspapermen and photographers invaded each of the sloops in turn eager to pump stories from men who could only blink red-eyed and sleepily as flash-bulbs exploded in their faces.

This was the price of carrying out the most successful patrol of the Battle of the Atlantic; no cruise before or since yielded such a triumphant victory for the Allies or dealt such a crippling blow to the U-boat Arm.[24] The Admiralty and the newspapers were determined to make the most of it for propaganda purposes.

In *Starling* Walker told Filleul to keep the Press at bay, instructed Eilleen to give no interviews and then escorted the First Lord and Sir Max to his cabin. Meanwhile, the fifty-one prisoners from *U-264* were marched ashore and handed over to an Army escort.

Presently a message was sent down to the wardroom asking Eilleen to join the group in the Captain's cabin and there she met Mr Alexander whose first words were:

'Well, Mrs Walker, we have already given your husband a CB and two DSOs, so what on earth do we give now? What would you suggest?'

'I really don't know,' replied Eilleen. 'But I am sure Johnnie isn't even thinking about it.'

On the dockside, a broad space had been cleared near the sloops whose crews were lined up in their respective divisions round a raised dais. From this Sir Max opened proceedings.

'I am proud of you all. This last voyage was a wonderful achievement. Here in Liverpool, we all watched your progress with mounting excitement. To say we were thrilled is putting it

---

[24] Three months later in the Pacific, the American aircraft-carrier *Hoggatt Bay*, with the anti-submarine vessels USS *England*, *George*, *Hazelwood* and *Roby* in company claimed six 'probable' Japanese submarines in a four-week cruise.

very mildly. Therefore on behalf of us all on the Staff ashore I thank you all for your good work.'

But more than anything else, the Group needed rest. While they tried to appear cheerful, many officers were too tired to drink the many toasts offered in their honour.

Walker and his family lunched in his cabin and helped to deal with fan mail. He received a surprising number of letters from people throughout Britain and even from America congratulating him and asking for advice on such problems as whether sons and daughters should join the Navy and the Wrens. He answered all these personally, particularly those from a Midland family named Starling.

After lunch, he said to Eilleen:

'Isn't it funny? All this fuss and ceremony and I'm still just the same old Johnnie they didn't think it worthwhile to promote.'

When homeward bound after leaving *Woodpecker* in the hands of the tug *Storm King*, Walker's officers had noticed that he was inclined to fret unduly about the date of their arrival in Liverpool. In that curious, inexplicable way by which news passes through ships, it was soon discovered that February 27th was his silver wedding anniversary.

Starling docked on the 25th and, after several furtive comings and goings by officers and ratings, Johnnie and Eilleen were invited on board for what was supposed to be a small anniversary party. It developed into a gay affair and on behalf of the Wardroom Filleul presented Eilleen with a silver dish suitably inscribed. Later, representatives of the ship's company came to present her with a silver sugar bowl and cream jug. Both gifts had to be made to her as it would have been a breach of regulations for the crew to offer a present to their captain.

About a week later, the value of the creeping attack came up again when Captain Pat Cooper arrived from London and dined aboard as Walker's guest. One of Walker's first antisubmarine pupils and now specializing for the Admiralty in new equipment, Cooper revived the idea that certain new equipment should be fitted in *Starling* and jokingly referred to her 'bow-and-arrow' instruments.

His arguments were useless. Walker's mind was set against anything new which could not be shown to have produced the same standard of success which he regarded now as normal. Cooper protested that this was almost impossible as the Second Support Group's record had not been equalled.

'Well, that's it,' Walker summed up. 'When I stop killing U-boats with my present set-up I shall come to you for something to cure the complaint. While I am successful, I honestly see no reason why I should clutter up the ship with a lot of gear which in all probability will never be used.'

When the two friends parted with a warning from Cooper that the latest instruments might yet prove valuable, neither could foresee that it was to be their last meeting. A friendship which had been born in the difficult days of Portland in the 'twenties, when all anti-submarine specialists were considered only one stage removed from cranks, was in its twilight.

But first the threat of the U-boat had to be stamped out to ensure free and unmolested passage across the battlefield for the great invasion convoys. Walker's tiring, lean, over-taut frame was being driven by seemingly boundless physical and mental energy. After hearing of an impudent U-boat which persisted in patrolling the mid-Atlantic, transmitting regular weather reports for the benefit of the Luftwaffe and Wehrmacht as well as the U-boat Arm, the Second Support Group sailed again early in March to deal with this enemy weather station and any other U-boat which might be sailing in what were now rightly regarded as Allied waters.

On the eve of sailing, Derby House informed Walker that he had been awarded his third DSO. Worth far more to him was the announcement that he had been awarded two years' extra seniority as Captain. In one stroke a grateful Admiralty had wiped out the past and placed him again among his teammates. Their Lordships had erased forever the old black mark, 'lacking powers of leadership'.

CHAPTER 15: A GIFT TO STALIN

The Group sailed with the aircraft-carrier *Vindex*, for mid-Atlantic, a sister sloop, *Whimbrel*, having joined as a replacement for the lost *Woodpecker*. It seemed that their hunt might well prove fruitless; one U-boat in the Atlantic being almost like the proverbial needle in a haystack.

To help, the Group had intercepted the U-boat's wireless signals on HF/DF and the search area was narrowed down to a few hundred miles after a week of hunting. Eventually, at dawn some two days later, their quarry was discovered in a copybook combined air-sea operation.

The Atlantic weather had turned nasty again and asdic conditions were not helped by the high-running seas. *Vindex* flew off her dawn patrol and after an hour the aircraft broke out of cloud directly above the U-boat, which had surfaced ten miles from the Group. She crash-dived on sighting the plane, but the sloops were already heading for the scene at full speed. The infallible *Wild Goose* made contact first and, after handing the echo to *Starling*, waited for Walker's order to begin the attack. As a preliminary, designed to force the enemy to dive deep, he took *Starling* in for a medium-depth pattern which should have pinned her down nicely for *Wild Goose*. Unfortunately for Wemyss and his crew, *Starling*'s pattern destroyed the enemy, much to Walker's personal astonishment. As it had become the Group's unwritten rule that the first ship to detect an enemy should have the privilege of opening the attack, he sent the following signal to *Wild Goose*:

'I am guilty of flagrant poaching. Very much regret my unwarrantable intrusion into your game.'

So *U-653* was sunk by what was merely intended to be a softener attack before hostilities opened in earnest.

When this success had been reported to the Commander-in-Chief, Western Approaches, and the Group had celebrated, orders were received to proceed with dispatch to Scapa Flow, main base for the Home Fleet. At once a crop of rumours spread through the sloops that something big was in the wind — something, for instance, like a Russian convoy.

On March 28th, *Starling*, *Wild Goose*, *Magpie*, *Wren* and *Whimbrel* sailed from Scapa to join two other Groups as escorts for the Russian-bound convoy JW58, which carried aircraft and guns for the Red Army and Air Force. Also in company were two old friends from the mid-Atlantic patrols, the aircraft-carriers *Tracker* and *Activity*, and the senior officer of the combined force was the Rear-Admiral in command of the cruiser *Diadem*, then a comparatively new ship and leader of the Tenth Cruiser Squadron.

To Walker, who assumed automatic command of the three escorting Groups of sloops and destroyers, it soon became apparent that their real task was to ensure the safe arrival in Russia of a huge four-funnelled American cruiser, the USS *Milwaukee*, which was placed in the centre of the convoy. It was a gift from President Roosevelt to the Russian leader as a token of the American people's appreciation of Red Army successes.

Although sailing with an American crew under the Stars and Stripes, she was under the care and protection of the Royal Navy until reaching Russia. Before leaving Scapa, Walker had been warned at a briefing conference that, whatever the fate of the rest of the force, *Milwaukee* had to reach Russia intact, as Mr Churchill thought it might prove more than a little embarrassing if he had to explain to the President and Stalin why this symbol of Soviet-American friendship lay undelivered at the bottom of the Arctic! The Admiralty and the various senior officers at Scapa Flow concerned with *Milwaukee*'s fate were fully aware of the responsibility. It was thought that the operation needed not only a large escort of powerful antisubmarine striking ships but also a senior officer of strong calibre and experience to discourage the enemy.

But if Walker was senior officer of the escorts, he was by no means in command of the entire force. This authority was vested in *Diadem* and, no matter how he tried, he could not extricate his ships from the welter of orthodox Fleet instructions which came from *Diadem*'s bridge.

Throughout the first day, batteries of signal lamps blinked from the big ships in the middle of which Walker tried to get permission to carry out a practice shoot. *Starling*'s Yeoman of Signals tried patiently to get a word in edgewise at the chattering *Diadem* for more than twenty minutes before Walker, red-faced with anger and thoroughly upset at the screening orders, told him to abandon the attempt and turned to Burn, acting as staff gunnery officer to the Group, to say: 'I'm sorry. I just can't seem to get a thing out of that ship.'

For the Group, these were strange waters. It was not too cold if the men kept themselves well wrapped up in their Arctic clothing, but the weather played havoc with the senses. There were only four hours' darkness for most nights and the days were strangely unreal with so much daylight and no twilight or dawn.

Atmospheric conditions distorted wireless beams and HF/DF interceptions of enemy signals were not only frequent but gave wildly inaccurate bearings. On the night of the 30th, *Starling* literally stumbled across a U-boat. They picked up asdic contact about a mile to starboard and attacked with two hurriedly fired patterns set to explode between 150 and 300 feet. There was a tremendous under-water explosion followed by a stream of oil, wreckage and dead bodies floating to the surface. *U-961*, a newly commissioned boat outward bound from Norway to the Atlantic on her first war patrol, and chiefly concerned with making a safe passage through the 'Rose Garden', as the Germans called the area south of Iceland where they often had a bad time, was destroyed without ever knowing what had hit her. It is certain she had no evil intention towards the convoy and probably had no idea she was anywhere near a force of warships. She took no evading action and, in Walker's words to his officers later: 'She was that rare thing these days — a genuine mug.'

On another night, Walker picked up radar contact with a U-boat two miles from him and, ordering the Group to form up on him, gave chase at full speed. The enemy ran away on the surface and was out of range at dawn, but carrier aircraft dived on her and scored direct hits. *Starling* picked up evidence of destruction a few minutes later.

By this time the Group had fallen well behind the convoy and, as they turned to catch up at full speed, visibility became astonishing. Tiny stakes sticking up like needles over the horizon showed the position of the convoy; as they closed the range, hulls of ships appeared as thin, grey pencils which grew larger until finally taking shape. At times the merchant ships seemed to be flying several feet above the water in a glassy, hazy mirage while, on occasion, the water turned upside down and the ships sailed on the tips of their masts. Snow squalls appeared frequently and with startling suddenness. They could be seen forming up miles away and racing across the sea like white blankets lowered to the surface from huge black clouds. Officers of the Watch found it broke the monotony by varying their zigzags to avoid the squalls.

The group had nearly taken up their proper stations again when *Wild Goose*, true to her old tradition, found good enough reason to break this unreal peace and indulge in a practice shoot. Commander Wemyss asked Walker for permission to fire his guns, a request which was passed on to *Diadem*. It was refused on the ground that a single shot fired within sight or sound of the convoy would be welcomed by all as a chance to loose off a magazine or two and thus create confusion.

No sooner had Walker regretfully repeated this decision to *Wild Goose*, than her guns blared viciously and little puffs of black smoke appeared low on the horizon. Almost at once an enemy aircraft was seen dancing just above the sea in a misty haze out of range of the sloop's guns. Undoubtedly the pilot was reporting the convoy to German headquarters in Norway, and wheels were turning to intercept and interrupt their peaceful passage. Undeterred, Wemyss signalled gleefully to Walker: *Practice shoot completed.* Shortly afterwards, fighters flown off from the two carriers dived on the enemy who vanished disconsolately into the watery haze.

This was only the beginning for the Fleet Air Arm. The weather deteriorated until solid squalls of snow, rain and hail spread across the sky. Huge hailstones whipped the faces of those on watch until it was impossible to look into the wind with open eyes. Yet through all this the aircraft took off on daily sorties against enemy shadowers.

During the next few days and nights the U-boats gathered for a mass attack. HF/DF interceptions came rapidly but Walker refused to use up time, energy and fuel in chasing them all. There were several nightly skirmishes but no major attack developed.

The force arrived off Vaenga Bay, the escort base near Murmansk, on April 4th and parted company with the convoy.

A Russian pilot was embarked in *Starling* to lead the Group into the anchorage and, to make matters difficult, he could speak not a word of English. The Engineer Officer, who had been to Russia once and claimed to speak the language, was sent for to ask the pilot how far it was to the Bay. With the pilot looking over his shoulder, he put a finger on the chart where Vaenga Bay was marked and uttered strange sounds supposed to be Russian for 'How far?' The Russian looked at him stolidly and said: 'Ugh'. The Engineer Officer repeated his verbal acrobatics and each time received the stolid, 'Ugh'. Eventually he left the bridge in disgust muttering angrily under his breath something about these 'ignorant blasted Russians'. After this the pilot navigated *Starling* by pointing in various directions and grunting in different tones.

When they had anchored safely, the problem arose of how to entertain the pilot. He was taken down to the wardroom and Walker started proceedings by offering him a glass of the most powerful and virulent gin on board in the hope that he might mistake it for bad vodka. The Russian gulped it down in one and shook his head in strong disapproval. John Filleul followed by handing him a glass of whisky which again vanished in one gulp followed by a vigorous shaking of the pilot's head. A variety of other drinks received the same reaction until it was time for dinner, and the officers, who had been matching the pilot's drinks, were in fine fettle. Language difficulties were fast disappearing and half-way through the meal most of the wardroom was gaily incoherent. Then it was noticed that their guest was looking sullen and unhappy; he had no drink. It fell to the Navigator to save *Starling*'s prestige. Clearing his throat he said loudly: 'Bring the pilot one of those half-crown bottles of cooking port.'

After downing the first glass of this real red infuriator, the guest rolled his eyes and licked his lips with joy; at last he had been given a drink suitable to the Russian palate. In ten minutes he finished the bottle, and a second vanished with equal speed and dexterity. Then, with some assistance, he made his way to the Captain's cabin and collapsed on the bunk, happily out to the world.

The Second Support Group's stay in Russia was brief and unexciting. They watched a concert put on by a Russian Naval theatrical company but there was little else to do, and the lack of such ordinary institutions as pubs, cinemas and dance halls proved an incentive to stay aboard.

Starling's officers had not yet visited the newcomer, *Whimbrel*, so with the pilot in company they proposed to call, taking care to warn the sloop in advance that cooking port was a 'must' for the guest. While in *Whimbrel*'s wardroom that night there was a sudden commotion on deck. A sailor, overcome with emotion at being so close to the birthplace of Communism, attempted to desert the Royal Navy to seek happier days in Stalin's ships. He had thrown a Carley raft overboard, jumped down into it and was paddling furiously for shore. *Whimbrel*'s crew lined the ship's side in awed silence to watch this performance. The would-be deserter had forgotten to let go the rope securing the raft to the ship and there he was, some twenty yards away, pulling the rope tight with long, powerful thrusts of the paddle while the raft stayed exactly in the same spot.

Eventually, several sailors hauled the raft slowly back to the ship, but the Red-minded seaman, intent on his paddling, failed to notice in the darkness that he was going backwards until the raft bounced gently against the ship's side and he turned to look up at his shipmates who were gazing down in sheer wonderment. There was a gale of laughter which echoed across the harbour as he was pulled aboard, crestfallen and angry, to face punishment.

There was nothing impressive about Russian life ashore. The value of money appeared to be nil and in consequence even the street urchins — of whom there were many — seemed to have plenty; fantastic prices were asked for chocolates and cigarettes but there was little else to buy.

During the voyage home there were no serious engagements with the enemy and Walker grumbled later that it was marked only by 'the humiliating experience of getting three U-boats by radar and visual sighting, only to get no asdic contact at all once they dived — conditions were so bad'. While the main force of warships broke away from the convoy they were escorting to head for Scapa Flow, Walker and his Group were ordered to return to Liverpool, where they arrived on April 14th.

At Derby House, Walker met several of the officers who had taken the USS *Milwaukee* to Russia and were then on their way back to the United States. When the Stars and Stripes had been lowered and the Red Flag hoisted in its place, the USS *Milwaukee* had become, in the official words: 'The first sea fighting Unit of the Union of Soviet Socialist Republics to be named the *Murmansk.'*

After a brief rest at home with Eilleen and Gillian, who stayed at 'The White House' when off duty, Walker was called back to sea again, this time to sail with *Tracker,* for final mopping-up operations prior to the invasion of Normandy. The main U-boat force was being pulled back into the Western Approaches, but the few still marauding along the convoy routes could inflict heavy losses on the pre-invasion build-up of supplies if allowed to operate unhindered. They had to be harried and chased until they withdrew to more favourable battlegrounds.

Walker seemed to be tanned and fit. The craggy jaw was, perhaps, a little craggier; the wide-set eyes more sunken than usual; and the crinkly, brown hair receding a bit from the forehead and showing the first signs of greyness at the temples. But the effect was that of an athlete at the peak of his training — that is, to anyone who didn't know him well. Possibly the only person who noticed these first signs of strain and weariness was Eilleen.

His energy was amazing, and unfortunate mistakes by the Group's commanding officers could bring either a witty, ready rejoinder or a biting blast from which the sting had been taken by his choice of language. His standing among the Liverpool authorities was higher than ever and this was amply illustrated when he showed his contempt for red tape by having *Starling's* 'foxer' anti-'gnat' device put ashore before the long trailing wires once fouled her propellers. The equipment was landed on the dockside with not a word of protest from Derby House.

Although it was known among the Staff ashore and the Group's officers that he was working hard and shouldering far more responsibility than his rank warranted, none of them could see that it was having any effect other than to stimulate him in his grim determination to help destroy the enemy. But the constant strain of being in the fight for longer than any other officer afloat was relentlessly taking toll of mind and body, wearing thin the machinery of his heart and gnawing at the delicate mechanism of the brain. Had he been given a shore appointment then, this story might have taken a very different course. There were few in those days who would have dared to try and part Walker from *Starling*, and it became a simple matter of how long he would last before some part of him collapsed.

On this voyage, surrounded by *Wild Goose, Magpie, Wren, Whimbrel* and *Tracker*, he cruised along the Atlantic battle front and, within a few days, was engaging the enemy in a final fight. The striking force reached their patrol area on May 1st, sighting only a large buoy bearing a tall mast-like affair which they had photographed before sinking it by gunfire. It looked as if the Atlantic had at last been freed of the U-boat pincers. But before this hope could settle into certainty, *U-473*, an impertinent 740-tonner carrying a crew of fifty-two, slunk across the black sea before dawn on May 3rd and sank the American destroyer USS *Donnell*, then about 20 miles southwest of the Group. Walker received news of this attack from Liverpool and further signals from the Admiralty gave the estimated position of the enemy according to interceptions of his radio chattering to France. He detached *Whimbrel* and *Magpie* to proceed at full speed to the assistance of the American warship and with *Wild Goose, Wren* and *Tracker* headed for the search area.

It was a classic hunt which took the Group back more than a year to their first scalp — *U-202*. That time it had taken nearly fifteen hours to destroy the enemy; this was going to take even longer.

Walker's instinct nosed out the U-boat. Although the enemy could have been almost anywhere inside a radius of 200 miles from the scene of the *Donnell* attack, he steered on what he hoped would be an interception course and proved right first time. Also in accordance with tradition, *Wild Goose* gained asdic contact first and carried out a swift anti — 'gnat' depth-charge attack before handing over the echo to Walker in *Starling*. *Tracker* was sent out of the danger area while the three sloops lined up for the run-in on a series of creeping attacks. At one time, *Starling* had to cut close to *Wild Goose*, and an angry voice bellowed from Wemyss' quarterdeck: 'Go find one of your own to play with. We started this little game and this time we want to finish it. Away with you.' There were grins in both ships which soon began to fade as one attack after another failed to produce evidence of destruction.

In *U-473* they had encountered a slippery opponent. He went on zigzagging steadily ahead with depth-charges falling about his ears and twice tried to escape by turning complete circles and reversing course in attempts to pass back between the sloops. Cunning as he was, hurried manoeuvres by the Group foiled each wriggle. So it went on all day and into the night.

This was, in fact, more of a repetition of the *U-202* hunt than had at first been thought possible. Nearly 900 feet — and the depth-charges were exploding well above. Walker decided to wait for him to surface through lack of air or run-down batteries, but towards midnight the enemy varied the depth and came up to fire a shower of 'gnats' in a vain chance of breaking up the hunting formation. *Starling* counter-attacked rapidly with twenty-six depth-charges which inflicted the first damage. After this Walker suspected he would surface at any moment.

U-473 came up shortly after midnight, the noise of blowing tanks heralding the battle's dramatic close to the waiting, listening Group. Starshell and flares silhouetted his tiny conning-tower as he attempted to run away at full speed. The three sloops, rolling horribly, opened fire with all they had as the enemy set off at a cracking pace across their bows. The water in the vicinity of the U-boat became a mass of foam as the combined fire fell around him; a salvo of four-inch guns from *Wren* struck home on the conning-tower; then two more from *Starling*, followed by excited claims over the R/T from *Wild Goose*.

Walker, always a spectator when the guns took over from his beloved depth-charges, clambered to the highest spot on the bridge and watched as an evil red glow spread from the conning-tower to the enemy's deck. Machine-gun tracer bullets streamed and bounced off armour plating in colourful fountains of light. On *Starling*'s bridge, Walker shouted above the sound of the salvoes:

'Come on, Burn. Give the blasted Boche hell.... Oh, well shot, someone, that's another direct hit.... We have got him this time.'

Through binoculars it was possible to see the U-boat's crew scamper from their action stations; then the gun on the foredeck vanished in a creamy whirlpool. Men were still manning the shattered stump of a conning-tower and, after twenty minutes of pitched battle, the victim turned towards her enemies, fired off a cloud of 'gnats' in a last desperate effort to take at least one of the sloops with him to the bottom. But the deadly torpedoes missed, the U-boat commander pointed his bows at *Starling* and lunged forward in a brave attempt to ram.

Walker stopped cheering suddenly and, with some alacrity, conned *Starling* out of danger only just in time. As the enemy passed across their bows another salvo from Wren crashed into him. It was the death blow. The crew were seen to leap overboard while *U-473* shuddered to a stop. Then with nose pointed downwards, it sank, leaving thirty of the crew to be picked up by *Starling* and *Wild Goose*.

Starling alone had fired nearly 150 rounds of ammunition. A few minutes later a signal was sent to Liverpool saying that U-

473, the sinker of the USS *Donnell*, had been destroyed and our Allies avenged.

The Group resumed patrolling but there was nothing to disturb the peace for the next few days and, somewhat bored, they set sail for home. If the battlefield remained quiet, it was not so peaceful in *Starling*. At dawn on the 8th a sentry, guarding the sleeping U-boat prisoners, fired his revolver accidentally and wounded a German in the left shoulder. The revolver, a six-shooter, had one chamber empty for safety. One sentry pulled the trigger to see if the chamber was empty. It was, so he handed it over to his relief, saying: 'It's quite safe. You pull the trigger and nothing happens.' But he had forgotten to reset the chambers. Later, the relief decided to find out for himself and pulled the trigger. The result was one wounded prisoner.

Fortunately, the wound was not serious, but Walker was worried that the incident might lead to a rash of atrocity stories in Germany with reprisals against Royal Navy prisoners. He sent for the German, apologized on behalf of the Navy and then asked the senior German prisoner aboard, who happened to be a petty officer, to sign a statement testifying that it had been an accident. While this was prepared, he held a quarterdeck inquiry which led to severe punishment for the sentry responsible.

On the 17th, the Group returned to Liverpool where Sir Max Horton was waiting impatiently to discuss the role of the Western Approaches Command in the coming Allied return to the Continent — the D-day landings.

Eilleen, who had thought for some time that her husband was overdoing it at sea, noticed now how haggard he had become. 'I was aghast,' she recalls, 'at the toll being taken of his strength and resistance.' Nevertheless, on that first night when his most urgent need was for sleep, he was summoned to Derby House to dine with the Commander-in-Chief and other senior officers. He returned home late, flopped on his bed and said:

'I'm all right, although I feel pretty tired now. You see, I stay on the bridge for as long as possible. I see the sailors looking up and know they are thinking: "It's all right, the old man's up there." It does give them confidence, you know.'

Then he added somewhat naively, and with boyish pride:

'As a matter of fact, I can stay on the bridge much longer than any of the young chaps.' That was the trouble; he could and did. As a result he was killing himself, gradually but inevitably.

The following day he was sent for again by Sir Max to be given the first indication of his future in the Royal Navy — as the Admiralty saw it.

'I think we are on top of this U-boat war at last, Walker,' said Sir Max, 'and it's largely due to your efforts.'

'Not all mine, Sir. The Group's as well.'

'That may be, but there is no need now to kill yourself over this business in the Atlantic. Bigger things are coming up. I have had a word with Their Lordships and it seems to have been decided that you should have a complete rest for two months after we have got our troops securely entrenched in Europe. That should be in about August. It won't be a desk job, but a proper rest.'

'I don't think that will be necessary, Sir. I feel fine and the Group have got used to me being around. I should like to finish the war with them. Then I can retire fairly gracefully.'

'I'm afraid not,' the Commander-in-Chief smiled. 'You are slated to take command of an aircraft-carrier to get you accustomed to air procedure and, somewhere about the end of the year, you will be promoted to Flag rank and given a carrier task force to take out to the Pacific. That war looks as though it might drag on for quite a while yet and there will be a real need for you out there. How does that sound?'

'Wonderful, Sir. But frankly I have been thinking seriously about retiring after the war and giving some time to my family, home and garden. I've had my share and it would be a waste for the Admiralty to promote me for the sake of a few months. Why not let me finish up doing the work I know best?'

'I'm sorry,' replied Sir Max, 'but I don't think the Admiralty will let you retire. You are too valuable an officer, Johnnie, and there is going to be a crying need for Admirals with your experience after the war. I'm afraid Their Lordships will insist you take both the promotion and the appointment, or else..... Anyway, think about it, and meanwhile I'll arrange for you to be sent on leave somewhere in August when the invasion business has sorted itself out.'

Walker repeated the conversation to his wife later that night and she was mostly relieved to hear that he was to be given a rest. But the more he talked the more upset he seemed to become.

'I told the Elephant[25] I wanted to retire when all this is over,' he said almost plaintively, 'but he said I could forget that as they would never let me go. Think of what a mess I shall make of the peacetime Navy.'

The matter was left in abeyance while he prepared for D-day.

---

[25] A Western Approaches nickname for the Commander-in-Chief.

CHAPTER 16: THE PRICE

For many weeks the ships of the Western Approaches Command had known that the invasion of Normandy might take place any day. What would be their role in that vast, cross-Channel armada? Their old adversary, Grand Admiral Doenitz, supplied the answer; he had devised a threefold counter to the invasion fleets which could be launched with deadly effect — if he were given enough time. His defence of the Occupied territories by the U-boat Arm called for:

> (1) The withdrawal of orthodox U-boats from the Atlantic battlefield for equipping with 'Schnorkel' breathing apparatus. This would allow them to move in Channel and coastal waters comparatively immune from air reconnaissance.
>
> (2) The massed counter-attacks by midget one-and two-man submarines hard to spot from the air, harder to hit even if sighted, and able to operate in those restricted waters which larger boats would be unable to penetrate. He could accept high losses in this weapon as the manpower was negligible and the tiny submarines were easy to mass-produce cheaply.
>
> (3) The introduction into the U-boat war of an entirely new boat of revolutionary design with which he hoped to cut the invasion supply lines, paralyse the invasion ports along the English coast and drive Allied shipping from the Atlantic highways.

It is reasonable to say today that this new boat might well have achieved all these aims had D-day been delayed for as little as weeks or had the invasion itself miscarried in some way. For these boats could maintain their surface speed while submerged at any depth and at twenty knots, carrying twice the normal number of torpedoes, could follow and attack the same convoy for the whole of its crossing from the United States to Britain. The destruction they could cause would be limited only by their fire-power. If detected, they could run away at a greater speed than most of the escort vessels, while in the Channel they could pass through an invasion supply fleet firing left and right and be gone before the slender escort had fully understood what had happened.

This was a development which if allowed to pass the final stages of experimental trials and go into production might well have changed not only the course of the war, but of history.

Fortunately for the Allies, the delay to D-day was counted in hours only and Doenitz was never given time to put these new boats on mass-production lines.

The Allies fully expected the still considerable might of the U-boat Arm to be flung against the cross-Channel supply lines; the enemy withdrawal from the Atlantic made it possible to release escort groups and striking forces to be deployed in the Channel, the southern Irish Seas and off the Biscayan coasts in waters which the enemy must cross to reach Normandy. These had been German-controlled since 1940 and the risk of losses due to enemy air action had to be accepted. To minimize the risk, the various Groups which had been operating together as teams for many years had to split up and re-form to ensure an even distribution of anti-aircraft guns.

More by example and personality than by orders, Walker had impressed upon his Group the action to be taken in almost any given emergency. No one in the Group wanted to fight under another leader. There was something deeper and more binding; with familiar ships around they felt secure and undismayed by danger because of the solid record of confident team work which had become the driving force behind their reputation of success. With it had come an unqualified trust between officers, men and ships. This would not be easy to replace.

With *Kite*, *Woodpecker* and *Woodcock* already lost to the Group, they were now to lose *Magpie* and *Whimbrel*, leaving only *Starling*, *Wild Goose* and *Wren* to carry on the tradition and pass it on, if possible, to the Group's recruits, *Loch Killin*, *Loch Fada* and *Dominica*, representatives of a new class of frigate and slightly smaller than the sloops.

Towards the end of May they sailed for an energetic battle course in the Irish Sea. Conditions they might expect to meet in the Channel fighting were simulated with the help of Fighter Command, a flotilla of submarines and one of motor torpedo boats. It was a dress rehearsal for the real thing and not a little frightening. It was not funny when a flight of cannon-firing fighters screamed down firing live ammunition into the water just ahead of the ships while they were allowed only to train their guns on the fighters. Under these realistic conditions accidents were inevitable and, if some were fatal, all were necessary.

After this livening-up period, the Group spent a few days at anchor in Lough Foyle waiting, as were thousands of other Allied fighting men around the coasts of Britain, for the signal to go. Ships' companies were trained to a fine pitch; further training would have made them stale like an overworked boatrace crew.

In the first days of June a general signal was received from the Admiralty instructing commanding officers to open the sealed orders for 'Operation Neptune', code name for the actual Normandy landing operations. This vast omnibus of orders included instructions for the Second Support Group to proceed to Moelfre Bay, south of Anglesey on the Welsh coast, to wait for the signal which would set off the greatest combined operation in history.

The function of the Western Approaches ships was to repel Doenitz's expected counter-attack. They were to gather at Moelfre Bay from where, on Walker's orders, the fleet of some forty-odd destroyers, sloops, frigates and corvettes would be thrown along patrol lines stretching from Brest to the Scilly Isles; and from Land's End to the Channel Islands.

It had been a fine summer's day when the Group sailed from Lough Foyle, but by the time they arrived at Moelfre Bay the wind had risen to gale force and the Western Approaches fleet was at anchor, half-hidden by flying spray and sleet. As Walker was senior officer, *Starling*'s motor-boat was sent round the ships distributing orders and collecting commanding officers for conferences during which loose ends were tied up and patrolling procedures worked out to provide an unbroken screen between the actual supply lines and the U-boat Arm. The gale kept up for another twenty-four hours until just as the keen, tensed-up crews thought the operation might be called off, the historic signal was sent which began the return journey to Europe.

Signals blinked from *Starling*'s bridge lamps and the Western Approaches men weighed anchor to sail for a new and much smaller battleground. From this day onward an even greater strain was to fall on Walker. Most of the ships were strictly convoy escorts which had operated in the limitless waters of the Atlantic for five long years. Their officers and men were accustomed to wide-open spaces with plenty of deep water and sea-room. Narrow waters strewn with wrecks, shoals and other navigational dangers were strange to them.

Similarly, the Coastal Command pilots who were to sweep ahead of the patrol lines to force the enemy to submerge were not the same experienced men who had flown over the Bay in the days of the blockade. They were mostly fresh to the U-boat war and keen as mustard — that was the trouble. Every swirl of water became a U-boat, every broom handle a periscope. As soon as the ships reached their patrol lines, reports flowed in of squadrons of U-boats flocking to the invasion area.

If many of these were false, there were plenty which proved accurate. Doenitz had counter-attacked. His new type of submerged speedboat submarine had not completed its trials, but with midget submarines from the northern French ports cooperating, he sent out his waiting fleets from Biscay to pierce the Channel defences.

On D-day, seventy-six U-boats sailed from their bases for the invasion area, mostly commanded by men who had operated in the Atlantic and had a natural preference for staying on the surface. 'Schnorkels' were ignored in their haste to deliver a crippling blow during the critical build-up period at the beach-heads. Instead, they met the full blast of Coastal Command's advance patrols. In the first twenty-four hours, while the surface units were forming up, thirty-six U-boats were sighted streaming towards the Channel, twenty-three being attacked and six sunk. U-boat commanders learned all about their 'breathing equipment' in double-quick time and the advance continued, but now underwater, as they crept towards the spread-out Groups waiting to fire a solid wall of depth-charges across the Channel entrances.

But if the enemy had in reality dived, Coastal Command insisted he was still on the surface, and the number of sightings increased until the patrols in the Channel bottleneck became one headlong chase after another. The ships packed into the area so complicated matters that two lines of ships going hell-for-leather after different aircraft sightings were frequently forced to cut through each other at acute angles. On one occasion Walker's Group had gained a contact at a point where two other Groups were crossing through each other. The subsequent melee as one force went into a prearranged circling movement to prevent the enemy escaping; and as two more ships ran in to attack while another force tried to clear the pitch — the whole affair being carried out in the darkness without lights — required something special in the way of good seamanship and alertness to avoid collision while at the same time destroying the enemy.

Under these conditions it was almost impossible for Walker to leave his bridge for any length of time. These were snags to be ironed out ashore and, as the senior officer of the patrolling forces, it was his job to recommend the answers when he returned to harbour for periodic conferences.

The Supreme Commander, General Eisenhower, had asked for the Channel to be kept clear of U-boats for at least two weeks while the armies secured a firm foothold on the Continent. Walker was determined he should get not only the two weeks, but that the U-boat Arm should be smashed for all time. He lived on his bridge at sea and, while others rested in harbour, he attended conferences. Then it was back to sea again for the same round of scares, alarms and false emergencies; the organizing of fruitless searches, the direction of several striking forces at the same time and the mental noting of all problems which could be solved if only someone ashore used a little sense.

During the first week, the U-boats failed to menace the landings, although a moment's relaxation might have been enough to allow a handful to get through and create chaos in the congested landing areas. The stakes were high; in these restricted waters the Western Approaches fleet faced the full strength of the U-boat Arm in direct and open conflict, the climax of a battle which for so long had stretched more than half-way round the world.

Walker took the Second Support Group into the front line between the Scilly Isles and Brest, prowling along the French coasts. On one such cruise, Filleul, on the morning watch, sighted another force of warships hunting dead ahead. It was still dark and obviously the Group would have to cut through. He called down the voicepipe to the captain's cabin.

'Ships dead ahead, Sir. We shall be going through them on this course.'

'Right, Number One,' came the sleepy reply and Filleul waited for his captain to guide the Group through the danger area. He waited, but Walker failed to arrive. He waited until the crisis moment when some action had to be taken to avoid collision. Then the young First Lieutenant made the necessary signals and took avoiding action, for the moment carrying the burden of responsibility for the safety of every ship in the Group.

Fortunately there were no mistakes, no collisions; and the following morning when Walker stumbled wearily to the bridge and asked cheerfully if everything were all right, John reported the incident with gentle reproach for having been left unexpectedly in command of the Group at such a moment. Walker remembered nothing about it; he could not recall being disturbed by his First Lieutenant's report; nor his own reply. It vaguely crossed Filleul's mind that his captain needed a good long rest.

Walker was his energetic self the next night when he led the Group in closer to the enemy coast than ever before, so close in fact that the German garrison at Ushant lighthouse signalled:

'Good evening. What ship?'

'Heil Hitler, you dirty —,' was Walker's reply. On *Starling's* bridge he muttered: 'That ought to make the Boche open fire on us.' But the enemy was probably too astonished to take such elementary action in retaliation for the insult and the night passed peaceably enough.

If Coastal Command had slowed down the U-boat advance during the first week, the surface units delivered their blow in the second. As the enemy moved slowly up the Channel, eight of his number were destroyed and the rest hugged the jagged coastline, using 'Schnorkels' to breathe and not daring to move until the surface was momentarily clear of Allied units. This was difficult, for the Navy's frantic hurryings hither and thither, as Commander Wemyss has since described it, made it seem to the miserable U-boats as though the sea were as full of destroyers as the air was of bombers.

General Eisenhower was given his two free weeks, not a single enemy penetrating through the invasion area. By the third week it was doubtful if Doenitz possessed the fifty-odd U-boats with which he had opened the war five years before, but he persisted in sending them all to sea. On the basis that, if they tried hard enough for long enough some would have to get through, he succeeded in making minor dents in our screen by D-day plus eighteen.

About this time, the Second Support Group, now joined by another frigate, *Lochy*, was carrying out a last sweep close to Ushant. It was a clear, sunny morning with a slight Channel mist hovering close over the shoreline. Suddenly a lamp blinked urgently from *Wren*: *Radar reports indicate twenty-one unidentified aircraft approaching. Range twenty-six miles.*

The aircraft were coming from the direction of France and it was logical to expect them to be Germans. Perhaps, thought *Starling's* officers, they were getting fed up with seeing the

Group so often on their doorstep at breakfast time. Then the aircraft came in sight, flying low over the coast straight towards the Group, not twenty-one as *Wren* had reported, but a vast black cloud of planes thundering through the air at high speed. As they came nearer, the cloud grew larger and the roaring louder, until it seemed that the sea quivered under the impact of violent sound. To the small ships below there could be no hope of surviving such a terrible onslaught.

Guns were trained round, and their crews sat wax-like and waiting for what appeared in every way to be the Group's final battle. While trigger fingers itched for the order to open fire, a calm voice came over the R/T to be heard by every ship:

'*Wren*, this is Captain Walker. I thought you said there were only twenty-one. It seems to me there might be a few more.'

For a moment there was a stunned silence on *Wren*'s bridge, then her captain, capturing the spirit of Walker's apparent indifference, replied delightedly:

'Sorry, Sir. My radar operator can't count over twenty-one.'

When each gunnery officer was about to give the order to commence firing, Walker's voice came over again:

'Do not open fire. Secure action stations. These aircraft are Flying Fortresses.'

It was almost possible to hear the sigh of relief which spread through the Group. Walker himself had placidly sat on *Starling*'s bridge throughout the entire affair eating a bacon and egg sandwich and drinking a cup of cocoa.

Shortly after this incident, he decided that the main battle would develop near the invasion areas, if it developed at all. *Starling* contracted an unexpected dose of 'condenseritis' and returned for repairs to Plymouth where it would be possible for the Captain to talk the Commander-in-Chief into giving his

Group a new patrol line in the vicinity of where a U-boat attack might be expected.

He succeeded in having the Group transferred and rejoined them in the Channel with the 'condenseritis' inexplicably cured again in a surprising manner. But the U-boats failed to make any concerted attack and the next week was marked by vain searches. One of these began with a series of underwater explosions ahead of the Group's hunting formation. They spent some time investigating without result until Walker called off his ships with the signal: *I am afraid we must leave it and put it down to an ichtheological gefuffle.*[26]

These days, *Starling's* officers began to see signs of strain in their captain. His keen, hazel eyes had lost their eager glint; the spare frame drooped slightly; and he no longer joined in the wardroom parties when in harbour, preferring to write letters home in his cabin.

Returning to harbour only increased his anxieties. While officers could relax, he was constantly attending conferences and courteously receiving the commanding officers of his ships who brought a continuous stream of problems for immediate decision.

On July 2nd, with ships and men worn out, the Group arrived in Liverpool for repairs and rest. No one, however, could foresee the blow about to fall. All signs pointed in a different direction; for it was announced that Captain F. J. Walker had been awarded a fourth DSO. Two weeks earlier, while her husband was at sea, an Admiralty representative had called on Eilleen to tell her that Johnnie was to receive another award prior to being transferred to a larger command. He insisted that on this occasion she would have to see the Press.

---

[26] A fishy disturbance.

According to persistent rumours he was to be made a Knight Commander of the Bath.

For the first few days in Liverpool, Walker was content to stay at home resting, tidying up his garden, joking with Gillian, playing with Andrew and telling Eilleen about his recent activities in the Channel. On July 7th, he went aboard *Starling* to hear a new recording of 'A-Hunting We Will Go' especially made by the band of the 2nd Battalion of the Manchester Regiment at the request of Bill Johnson. At lunchtime, Commander Wemyss came to say good-bye as *Wild Goose* was going into dock for urgent major repairs and the rest of the Group were expected to sail again within the next forty-eight hours.

They chatted in Walker's cabin of triumphs and troubles they had shared and, before Wemyss left, a signal arrived ordering the Group to sea the following evening.

Captain and Mrs Walker met several of the *Starling*'s officers for lunch at the Adelphi Hotel. Bill Johnson was unusually quiet and over coffee handed his captain a letter received in *Starling* that morning. It was from the Admiralty and contained confirmation of Timothy's death a year before in *Parthian*.

Although they were now used to the idea that Timothy was dead, the official terms of the letter made everything very final. Walker told his officers to be ready to sail and left the hotel with Eilleen.

That afternoon, they went to see a film called *Madame Curie*. On the way back, Walker started complaining of giddiness and curious humming noises in his head. At home, he was violently sick and the giddy spells recurred. Eilleen, who had rarely in her life heard him complain of any illness, rang up Captain (D) and arrangements were made for Walker to be examined at the Royal Naval Hospital, Seaforth, where he was seen by

Lieutenant-Commander C. A. Clarke, RNVR, and sent to bed. Eilleen was told not to worry. Her husband was very tired and in need of rest.

During the next day it became quickly apparent that something serious was wrong with Johnnie Walker. The sudden shock that perhaps his life was in danger spread from Eilleen to Sir Max Horton and through the entire Command. In the evening, Eilleen was summoned to his bedside. Now, as he lay weak with fast-fading strength, he was content again to have her sitting beside him quietly saying her rosary.

At midnight, he fell asleep and a naval car took Eilleen home. Two hours later, on Sunday the 9th, Captain Walker was dead.

According to the doctor he had died of cerebral thrombosis. In fact, he died of overstrain, overwork and war weariness; body and mind had been driven beyond all normal limits in the service of his country. The message informing the Admiralty said formally: 'Captain Walker's death is considered to be aggravated by and attributable to the conditions of his Naval Service.'

The Second Support Group were steaming into the Channel battlefield during the middle watch in Walker's favourite hunting formation, line abreast and a mile apart. It was nearly 3 am when an Admiralty signal was simultaneously received in all ships:

> The Admiralty regrets to inform you of the death of your Senior Officer, Captain F. J. Walker, which took place at 0200 today.

Walker's own 'gallant *Starling*' was stunned by shock: at dawn the Ensign was half-masted and lifelines were trailed over the side in an ancient mariner's tribute to a dead hero, while upon the entire Group fell a strange hush of mourning. From ordinary seaman to captain they grieved over the loss of not only a leader, but a friend. Numbing shock seemed to hang over the Group like a pall; it was almost impossible to imagine the ships going into action without that tall, lean figure in the grey pullover and patch work waistcoat standing on *Starling*'s bridge eating a sandwich while he destroyed a U-boat; grinning when he missed; shouting orders over the loudhailer as his 'chicks' got mixed up in an attack; cheering wildly when guns blazed at a tiny conning-tower silhouetted in the silvery moonlight; meting out stern punishment at the defaulters' table; and standing on his head in the wardroom with a glass of beer.

Officers and men repeated again and again, as though by some miracle it might not be true: 'The Captain is dead.'

Signals of sympathy poured into Derby House and the copies were sent by hand to Eilleen at 'The White House'. That Captain Walker served not only England, but all the Allies, was underlined in a signal from Admiral Stark.

> The United States Forces in Europe wish to convey their deepest sympathy in the loss of an outstanding fighting naval officer in the untimely death of Captain Walker. Although this, loss will be keenly felt by all the Allied forces everywhere, his fighting spirit will endure with us.

Alongside Gladstone Dock, overlooking the Mercy, was the tiny Flotilla Chapel where once Walker had read the lessons at Sunday services. Here, on the morning of the nth, the crests of the Western Approaches Battle Fleets looked down upon the body of Johnnie Walker resting in a coffin draped with the Union Jack.

Throughout the day sailors of all ranks came to kneel and pay silent homage to the man regarded by them all as not only a great leader and gallant officer, but always a distinguished gentleman. Outside, the business of war went on; the merchant ships shepherded by eager little tugs, the rust-streaked destroyers, sloops and frigates steaming wearily home from another grim struggle across the vast sea; and the smarter, gleaming warships proudly leaving harbour after refits to fill the gaps in the thin grey line.

The following morning, Nicholas and senior officers of the Command attended an intimate service in the Chapel, held by the Reverend J. Buckmaster, and later the body was taken to the steps of Liverpool Cathedral. Six petty officers bore the coffin up the steps between lines of ratings and laid it gently to rest in the choir where a blue-jacket guard of honour stood with reversed arms at each corner.

The Dean, Dr F. W. Dwelly, conducted a short service of Preparation of Resting and candles were lit to throw a pale glow over the single wreath lying on the flag-draped coffin and the hundreds of others massed in tiers in front of the choir — blue floral anchors, chaplets and circlets of bloom in all colours from the convoy ports, high-ranking Allied officers, ships' companies, individual officers and ratings, and from the shipping companies whose cargoes and ships had been saved by one man and his team.

In the afternoon, more than a thousand people, men and women of the Fighting Forces and civilians, crowded into the cathedral for the funeral service — still remembered as one of the most moving ever held in tribute to the memory of an active service officer.

Against the soft background of organ music, Admiral Sir Max Horton, who now reproached himself bitterly for not insisting that Walker take a rest ashore, read a Solemn Acknowledgement. The Cathedral was hushed while he spoke quietly:

'In the day when the waters had well-nigh overwhelmed us, our brother here departed, apprehending the creative power in man, set himself to the task to conquer the malice of the enemy. In our hour of need he was the doughty protector of them that sailed the seas on our behalf. His heart and his mind extended and expanded to the utmost tiring of the body even unto death; that he might discover and operate means of saving ships from the treacherous foes. Truly many, very many, were saved because he was not disobedient to his vision.

'Victory has been won and should be won by such as he. May there never be wanting in this realm a succession of men of like spirit in discipline, imagination and valour, humble and unafraid. Not dust, nor the light weight of a stone, but all the sea of the Western Approaches shall be his tomb.'

To the singing of 'Abide with Me', the flag-draped coffin was borne slowly out of the Cathedral by six petty officers flanked by eight ranking captains of the Command with gold-hilted swords held tightly to the waist and clear of the ground. Eilleen, Nicholas and Gillian followed — Andrew was too ill at the time to come — and then hundreds of sailors and Wrens fell in behind. At the bottom of the steps, the coffin was placed on a gun carriage and the cortege marched through the streets of Liverpool for the docks, where the body was taken aboard the destroyer *Hesperus*, for burial in the seas Captain Walker had known so well.

When the chief mourners had taken their places on the quarterdeck the tattered Battle Ensign from *Starling* was hoisted to half-mast and *Hesperus* slipped her moorings for the voyage down the Mersey.

Ships of all shapes and sizes dipped their ensigns in salute. Out to sea by the Bar Light Vessel — the light whose beam had cast warmth on so many battle-weary convoys — a convoy was entering harbour down one side of the channel as another was leaving. *Hesperus* steamed between the two lines of ships and the merchantmen lowered their ensigns while their crews stood bareheaded in a last salute to the man who had swept the Atlantic free of the enemy.

In the late afternoon, the destroyer reached the edge of the great, rolling ocean and here, under a darkening sky with the wind strong enough to fleck the grey-green waves with white, the weighted coffin was tilted over the side into the waiting sea.

EPILOGUE: *STARLING*

The death of Johnnie Walker paralysed *Starling*; a sudden wave of apathy and disillusionment swept through the ship, although little was said and the daily routine went on without apparent interruption. On deck, the guns' crews lay around their guns, the lookouts came and went, and the quartermasters put the ship through interminable zigzags. Signal lamps flashed and messages went to and fro. Outwardly, it was the same *Starling*, but the usual chatter and light-hearted chaff were missing; even the grumblers were silent. The petty officer often had to repeat a man's name before he answered. During drills reports were mumbled and slow where before they had been snapped in rapid, staccato precision; instruments which the men could normally operate in their sleep were handled as though by greenhorns.

It was unanimously thought that the only officer who could step into Walker's shoes with any certainty of immediate respect would be John Filleul who had served under him for so long that he reacted instinctively to emergencies in the Walker manner. But he was still young and too junior for promotion. A new captain was appointed and *Starling* went to sea. A month later the captain left the ship having contracted lumbago in Walker's leaky old sea cabin.

Wild Goose had not yet finished her refit, so Commander Wemyss, Johnnie Walker's right-hand man for more than a year and the Group captain closest to him, showed his understanding of *Starling*'s dilemma by going aboard and addressing the ship's company.

Then, seizing the opportunity to snap *Starling* out of her apathy, he took temporary command of both her and the Group for the next trip. The Walker tradition returned, with a difference. Once they had fought because it was their duty and expected of them; now the tussle became a grim vengeful battle to exact personal revenge for the death of their captain.

They were not long in finding the enemy. *Loch Killin* made contact off the French coast and dropped the usual anti — 'gnat' pattern of depth-charges. Suddenly, a U-boat surfaced directly beneath the startled frigate, eventually coming up with a rush to lock herself against *Loch Killin*'s quarterdeck. To the utter astonishment of the watching Group, the U-boat was literally hanging on the frigate's stern.

The Germans rushed to the conning-tower and turned to gaze open-mouthed at the depth-charge crew and put their hands above their heads as they stepped across the narrow gap on to *Loch Killin* and into captivity. A few minutes later, *Loch Killin* shook her tail free of the unwelcome stranger which sank immediately but only after her entire crew of fifty-two had crossed over to the frigate without getting their feet wet. One of *Starling*'s crew shouted excitedly:

'I bet the Old Man's rubbing his hands up there.'

They sank three more of the enemy before the patrol ended and the Group returned to Plymouth where Wemyss transferred back to *Wild Goose*. *Starling* went into drydock at Newcastle and the crew were paid off to disperse to other commands. She was still under repair when the war ended.

Neither she nor Walker will be forgotten. Recently her cracked ship's bell was auctioned and, despite a large bid for HMS *Osprey* who wanted it for their war museum, Commander Wemyss and several later captains of *Starling* clubbed together to present the bell to Eilleen, now living in Devon. When the

Captain of *Osprey* heard about this he withdrew his bid. *Osprey* remembers Walker in other ways; a street in the newly-built Naval Housing Estate is named 'Walker Crescent'.

Johnnie Walker died when not quite forty-eight. Yet he lived long enough to achieve his ambition — to help defeat the enemy. The official record of the Battle of the Atlantic pays the simple final tribute:

> The Royal Navy and the nation sustained a great loss in the death of Captain Frederic John Walker.... A prime seaman and fighter and a brilliant leader, he was without doubt one of the outstanding and inspiring figures of the anti-submarine war.

A NOTE TO THE READER

If you have enjoyed this book enough to leave a review on **Amazon** and **Goodreads**, then we would be truly grateful.
The Estate of Terence Robertson

Sapere Books is an exciting new publisher of brilliant fiction and popular history.

To find out more about our latest releases and our monthly bargain books visit our website:
saperebooks.com

Made in the USA
Columbia, SC
15 November 2023